www.booksbyboxer.com

No part of this publication may be reproduced or transmitted in any form or by any means, electronic or mechanical, including photocopying, recording or any information storage and retrieval system, or for the source of ideas without written permission from the publisher.

Bee Three Publishing is an imprint of Books By Boxer
Published by
Books By Boxer, Leeds, LS13 4BS UK
Books by Boxer (EU), Dublin, D02 P593, IRELAND
Boxer Gifts LLC, 955 Sawtooth Oak Cir, VA 22802, USA
© Books By Boxer 2024
All Rights Reserved
MADE IN CHINA
ISBN: 9781915410528

This book is produced from responsibly sourced paper to ensure forest management

GO FROM SIPPER TO SOMMELIER

Welcome to the exhilarating world of wine! Whether you're a casual sipper or an aspiring sommelier, this book is your passport to exploring the depths of viniculture, from the vineyards to the tasting room.

This journey isn't just about acquiring knowledge; it's about savoring the experience and cultivating a deep appreciation for the nuances of wine. From swirling and sniffing to sipping and savoring, we'll hone our senses and refine our palates, one glass at a time!

AGE IS JUST A NUMBER.
IT'S TOTALLY IRRELEVANT UNLESS, OF COURSE, YOU HAPPEN TO BE A
BOTTLE OF WINE.
- JOAN COLLINS

ALBARIÑO | BERRY SKIN WHITE
GALICIA (SPAIN)

A beautifully sharp and fruity Spanish white, Albariño is a coastal wine grown on the Iberian Peninsula. It is a great alternative to Sauvignon Blanc and Pinot Grigio for a mineral and crisp wine that is filled with fruit flavors!

PRIMARY FLAVORS:

LEMON ZEST — GRAPEFRUIT — HONEYDEW MELON — NECTARINE — APPLE

AROMAS:
Lemons, Limes, Pear, Granite, Peach.

FINISH:
Long, mineral finish.

PAIRS WELL WITH:
Light Meats, Burrata, Oysters.

TASTE PROFILE:

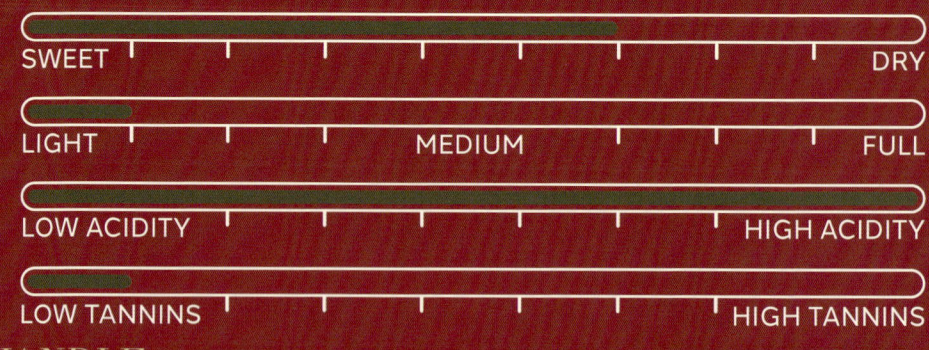

SWEET ———————————————— DRY
LIGHT ———————————————— FULL
LOW ACIDITY ———————————————— HIGH ACIDITY
LOW TANNINS ———————————————— HIGH TANNINS

HANDLE:

 **SERVE** 38–45°F / 3–7°C

GLASS TYPE Standard White

 **DECANT** No

 **CELLAR** 3–5 years

FAMOUS FOR:
A BRIGHT AND ZIPPY ALTERNATIVE TO PINOT GRIGIO AND SAUVIGNON BLANC.

WE RECOMMEND:
Citizen Wine Sand Boy Albariño 2022

GRAPES:
Albariño

REGION:
Rías Baixas, Spain

WINE STYLE:
White

ALCOHOL CONTENT:
12%

PRICE:
£15-£18 | $19-$22

WHERE IT GROWS:

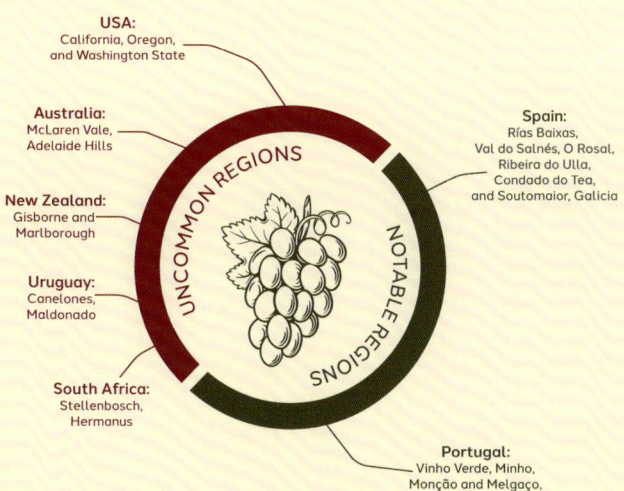

USA: California, Oregon, and Washington State

Australia: McLaren Vale, Adelaide Hills

New Zealand: Gisborne and Marlborough

Uruguay: Canelones, Maldonado

South Africa: Stellenbosch, Hermanus

Spain: Rías Baixas, Val do Salnés, O Rosal, Ribeira do Ulla, Condado do Tea, and Soutomaior, Galicia

Portugal: Vinho Verde, Minho, Monção and Melgaço,

UNCOMMON REGIONS | NOTABLE REGIONS

BACCHUS | BERRY SKIN WHITE
ENGLAND/GERMANY

Known for its semi-dry mouthfeel and complex aromas, Bacchus was grown in Germany in the 1930s, where the grape was known as a Riesling's less popular, sweeter cousin. The British climate has since produced more acidic and fresh grapes that tend to highlight the more subtle notes of the wine.

PRIMARY FLAVORS:

APPLE	BLOSSOM	CITRUS	HONEYSUCKLE	PEAR

AROMAS:
Elderflower, Green Pepper, Thyme, Basil, Lemon.

FINISH:
Crisp and dry.

PAIRS WELL WITH:
White Fish, Pork, Crab.

TASTE PROFILE:

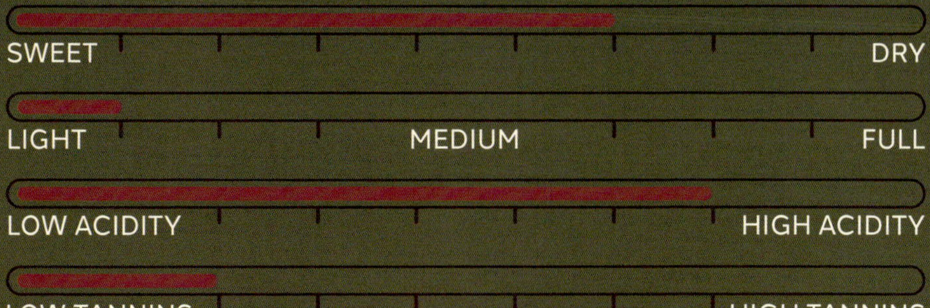

SWEET ———————————————————— DRY

LIGHT ———————— MEDIUM ———————— FULL

LOW ACIDITY ———————————————————— HIGH ACIDITY

LOW TANNINS ———————————————————— HIGH TANNINS

HANDLE:

 **SERVE** 45°F-50°F/ 7°-10°C

 **GLASS TYPE** Universal

 **DECANT** 15-30 mins

 **CELLAR** 3-5 years

FAMOUS FOR:
COMPLEX AROMAS, LIGHT COLORATION AND FRUITY, CITRUS FLAVOR.

WE RECOMMEND:
Beacon Down Vineyard Bacchus 2022

GRAPES:
Bacchus

REGION:
Kent, England

WINE STYLE:
White

ALCOHOL CONTENT:
11.5%

PRICE:
£15-£20 | $20-$25

WHERE IT GROWS:

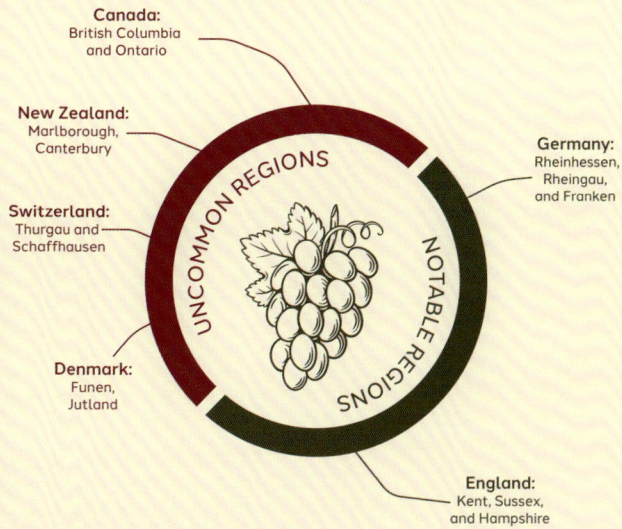

Canada: British Columbia and Ontario

New Zealand: Marlborough, Canterbury

Switzerland: Thurgau and Schaffhausen

Denmark: Funen, Jutland

Germany: Rheinhessen, Rheingau, and Franken

England: Kent, Sussex, and Hampshire

BANDOL | BERRY SKIN RED
SOUTHERN FRANCE

Bandol is a rich red produced in the Bandol region of Provence, France. Robust and fruity, Bandol is famous for its earthy spices and punchy flavor, and is an interesting alternative to a Shiraz, perfect for those who like punchy reds!

PRIMARY FLAVORS:

  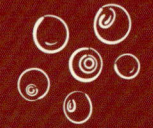  

BLACKBERRY — CHERRY — WHITE PEPPER — ANISE — DARK CHOCOLATE

AROMAS:
Berry, Tobacco, Cured Meats, Cherry, Lavender.

FINISH:
Long and structured.

PAIRS WELL WITH:
Roasted Leg of Lamb, Manchego.

TASTE PROFILE:

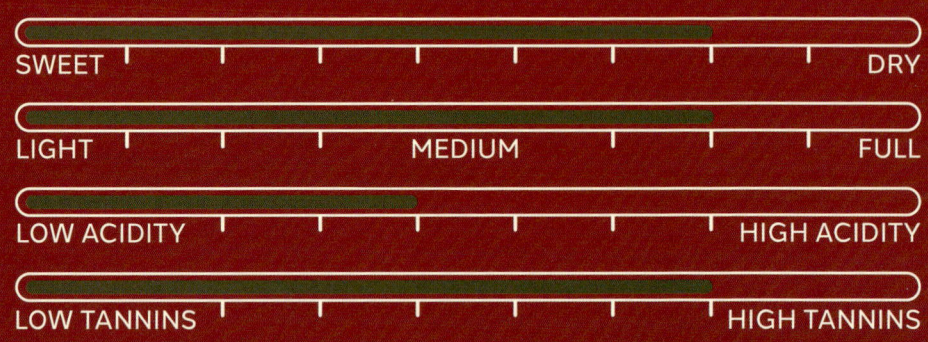

SWEET — DRY
LIGHT — MEDIUM — FULL
LOW ACIDITY — HIGH ACIDITY
LOW TANNINS — HIGH TANNINS

HANDLE:

 **SERVE** 60°F-65°F / 15°C-18°C

 **GLASS TYPE** Burgundy

 **DECANT** 1-2 hrs

 **CELLAR** 5-10 years

FAMOUS FOR:
ITS COMPLEX FLAVORS, RICH TEXTURE AND DEPTH OF CHARACTER.

WE RECOMMEND:
Domaine de la Bégude Rouge 2017 Vin rouge de Bandol AOC Bouteille

GRAPES:
Mourvedre, Grenache

REGION:
Provence, Southeastern France

WINE STYLE:
Red

ALCOHOL CONTENT:
13.5%

PRICE:
£24-£35 | $25-$45

WHERE IT GROWS:

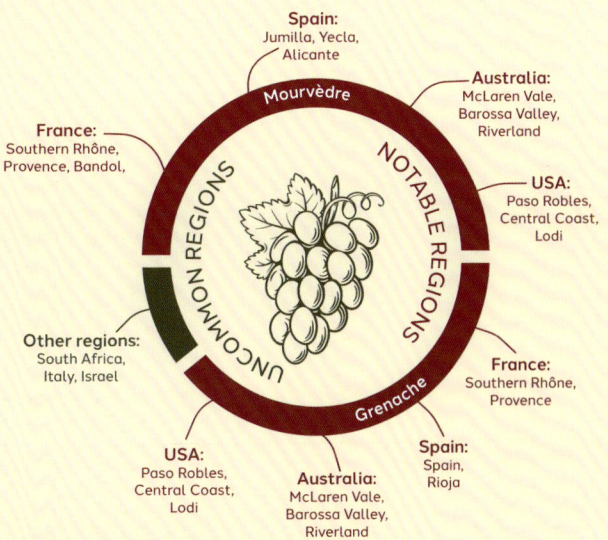

TYPES OF WINE GLASSES

The size and style of your glass is important in determining how you taste and smell the wine. Each wine has a preferred glass in order to maximize the experience!
I mean, prosecco out of a mug just wouldn't be the same...

• RED WINE:

BURGUNDY PINOT NOIR LARGE BORDEAUX CABERNET SAUVIGNON STANDARD RED

• WHITE WINE:

SAUVIGNON CHARDONNAY RIESLING SWEET MONTRACHET

• DESSERT WINE:

SAUTERNES PORT MADEIRA STANDARD SWEET SHERRY

• SPARKLING WINE:

VINTAGE TULIP FLUTE

• MISCELLANEOUS:

ROSÉ HOCK ALSACE TUMBLER

BAROLO | BERRY SKIN RED
PIEDMONT, ITALY

Produced predominantly in the Piedmont region of Italy, Barolo is characterized by its brick-red color, with intense and complex flavors that, despite being full bodied, flavors light on the palate.

PRIMARY FLAVORS:

CHERRY    RASPBERRY   PEPPER   ANISE    ROSE

AROMAS:
Strawberry, Rose, Cinnamon, Tar, Cherry.

FINISH:
Long and tannic.

PAIRS WELL WITH:
Truffle, Aged Cheese, Tortellini.

TASTE PROFILE:

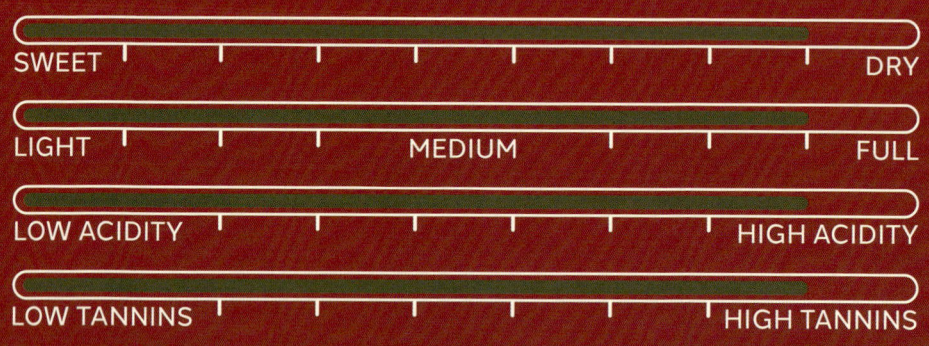

HANDLE:

 **SERVE** 60-65°F/ 15-18°C

 **GLASS TYPE** Burgundy

 **DECANT** 1 hr

 **CELLAR** 5-10 years

FAMOUS FOR:
A BRIGHT AND ZIPPY ALTERNATIVE TO PINOT GRIGIO AND SAUVIGNON BLANC.

WE RECOMMEND:
Tenuta Cucco Barolo del Comune di Serralunga d'Alba

GRAPES:
Nebbiolo

REGION:
Piedmont, Italy

WINE STYLE:
Red

ALCOHOL CONTENT:
14%

PRICE:
£18-£24 | $25-$35

WHERE IT GROWS:

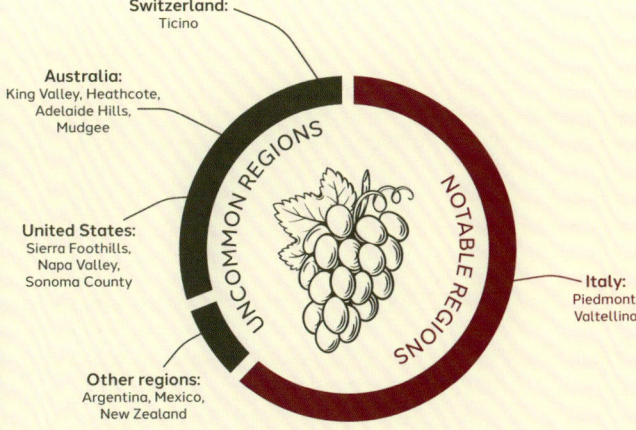

Switzerland: Ticino

Australia: King Valley, Heathcote, Adelaide Hills, Mudgee

United States: Sierra Foothills, Napa Valley, Sonoma County

Other regions: Argentina, Mexico, New Zealand

Italy: Piedmont, Valtellina

UNCOMMON REGIONS | NOTABLE REGIONS

CARMÉNÈRE | BERRY SKIN RED
BORDEAUX, FRANCE

Originating in Bordeaux, but now almost exclusively grown in Chile, this unique tasting wine is celebrated for its mouth-watering red and black fruit flavors, and distinctive green bell pepper and black peppercorn notes!

PRIMARY FLAVORS:

 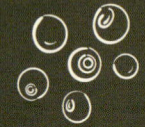  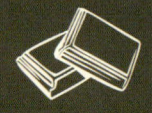 

PLUM   PEPPER CORN   GREEN PEPPER   DARK CHOCOLATE   CHERRY

AROMAS:
Blackberry, Clove, Plum, Coffee.

FINISH:
Smooth and velvety.

PAIRS WELL WITH:
Aged Cheese, Sirloin Steaks, Chimichurri.

TASTE PROFILE:

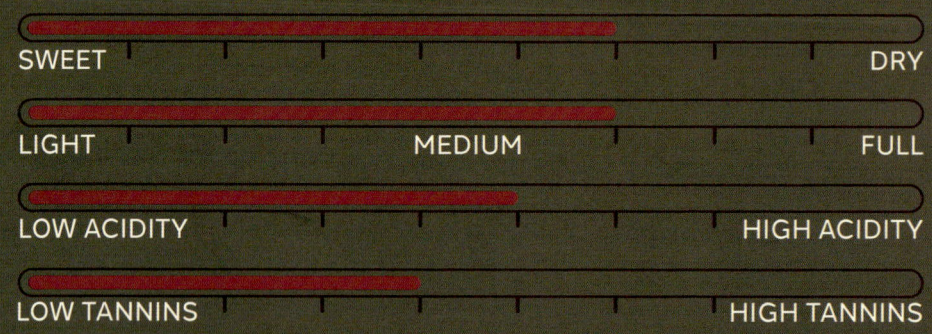

SWEET — DRY
LIGHT — MEDIUM — FULL
LOW ACIDITY — HIGH ACIDITY
LOW TANNINS — HIGH TANNINS

HANDLE:

SERVE
60-65°F/
15-18°C

GLASS TYPE
Burgundy

DECANT
30-60 mins

CELLAR
3-5 years

FAMOUS FOR:
UNIQUE GREEN BELL PEPPER NOTES AND A RED FRUIT-FORWARD TASTE.

WE RECOMMEND:
Tarapacá Gran Reserva Carmenère 2021

GRAPES:
Carmenère

REGION:
Maipo Valley, Chile

WINE STYLE:
Red

ALCOHOL CONTENT:
14%

PRICE:
£15 - £18 | $19-$22

WHERE IT GROWS:

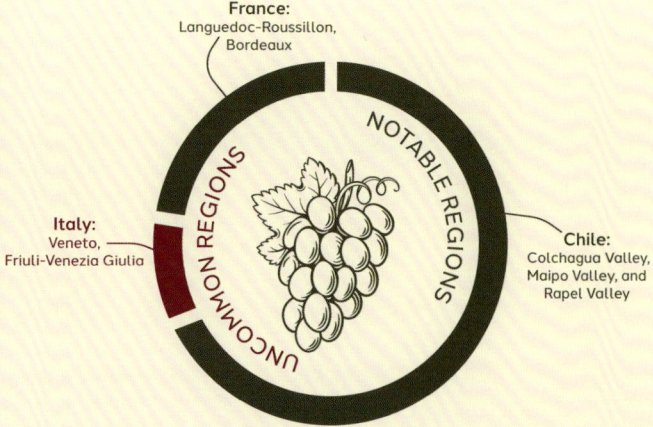

France: Languedoc-Roussillon, Bordeaux

Italy: Veneto, Friuli-Venezia Giulia

Chile: Colchagua Valley, Maipo Valley, and Rapel Valley

CHABLIS | BERRY SKIN WHITE
BURGUNDY, FRANCE

Made in the Chablis region of Burgundy, France, Chablis is usually made from Chardonnay grapes, giving it a fruity minerality and light to medium body. Chablis offers a wine that is similar to Chardonnay, but lighter due to its unoaked nature!

PRIMARY FLAVORS:

GREEN APPLE  **LIME** **PEAR** **WHITE FLOWER** **HONEYSUCKLE**

AROMAS:
Lemon, Lime, Pear, White Peach, Wet Stone.

FINISH:
Long and refreshing.

PAIRS WELL WITH:
Oysters, Crab, Smoked Salmon.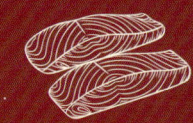

TASTE PROFILE:

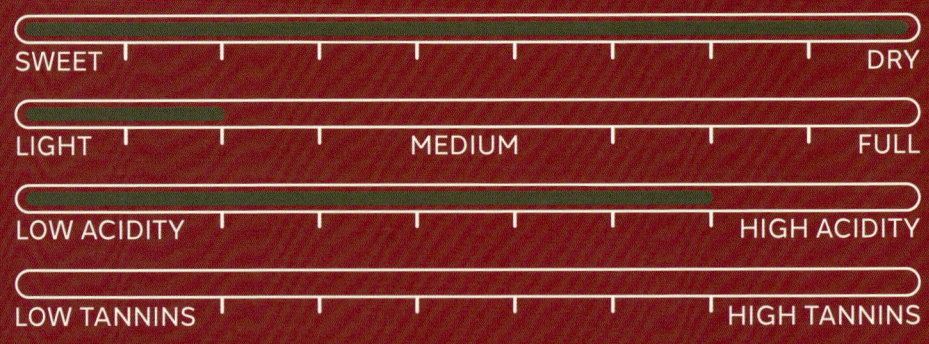

HANDLE:

SERVE
45–55°F/
7–12°C

GLASS TYPE
Standard
White

DECANT
No

CELLAR
3-7 years

FAMOUS FOR:
BEING AN UNOAKED, CRISP CHARDONNAY ALTERNATIVE.

WE RECOMMEND:
Domaine de la Motte Chablis 2022

GRAPES:
Chardonnay

REGION:
Burgundy, France

WINE STYLE:
White

ALCOHOL CONTENT:
13%

PRICE:
£19-£22 | $25-$28

WHERE IT GROWS:

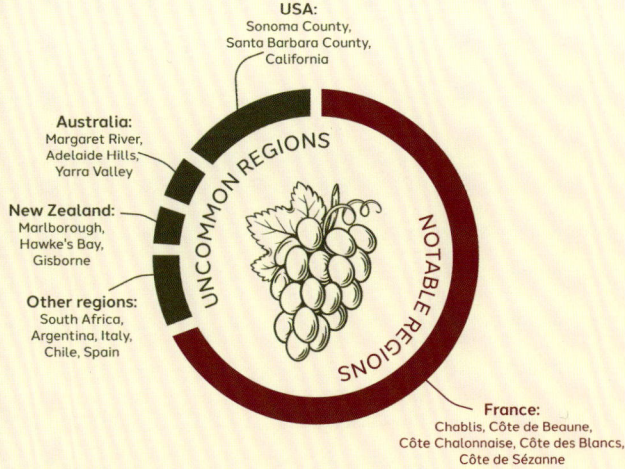

USA: Sonoma County, Santa Barbara County, California

Australia: Margaret River, Adelaide Hills, Yarra Valley

New Zealand: Marlborough, Hawke's Bay, Gisborne

Other regions: South Africa, Argentina, Italy, Chile, Spain

France: Chablis, Côte de Beaune, Côte Chalonnaise, Côte des Blancs, Côte de Sézanne

UNCOMMON REGIONS | NOTABLE REGIONS

- 17 -

TOP 5 MUST KNOW WINE REGIONS

TUSCANY, ITALY

Tuscany's rich history, stunning landscapes, and world-class wines make it a must-visit destination for wine lovers and travelers alike.

GRAPE VARIETIES:
Tuscany is renowned for its red wines, primarily made from Sangiovese, a versatile grape variety that thrives in the region's climate and soils. Other grape varieties grown in Tuscany include Cabernet Sauvignon, Merlot, and Syrah for red wines, and Trebbiano and Vermentino for white wines.

MOST PRESTIGIOUS WINES:
Chianti Classico, located in the heart of Tuscany, Brunello di Montalcino is produced exclusively from Sangiovese grapes grown in the hills surrounding the town of Montalcino. Vino Nobile di Montepulciano is made primarily from Sangiovese grapes grown in the vineyards surrounding the town of Montepulciano.

KEY WINE REGIONS:
Tuscany is home to several prominent wine regions, including Chianti, Brunello di Montalcino, and Vino Nobile di Montepulciano. Each region has its own unique terroir, grape varieties, and winemaking traditions, producing distinctive styles of wine.

TERROIR:
Tuscany's terroir encompasses a rich tapestry of climatic, geological, and geographical factors that shape the character and quality of its wines.

FOOD PAIRING:
Tuscan wines pair beautifully with the region's cuisine, which includes hearty dishes such as pasta with tomato sauce, grilled meats, wild boar stew, and pecorino cheese.

I COOK WITH
Wine,
SOMETIMES I EVEN ADD IT TO THE FOOD.

– W.C. Fields

CHIANTI | BERRY SKIN RED
TUSCANY, ITALY

This classic and well-known Italian grape originated in Tuscany, and is an essential in any Italian cooking – for both the food and the glass! With sweet but savory notes, Chianti is a versatile wine that accompanies meats, cheeses, and salads beautifully.

PRIMARY FLAVORS:

CHERRY — PLUM — STRAWBERRY — TOMATO — BALSAMIC

AROMAS:
Cherry, Oregano, Leather, Raspberry, Soil.

FINISH:
Fruity and lingering.

PAIRS WELL WITH:
Beef, Parmigiano-Reggiano, Pasta.

TASTE PROFILE:

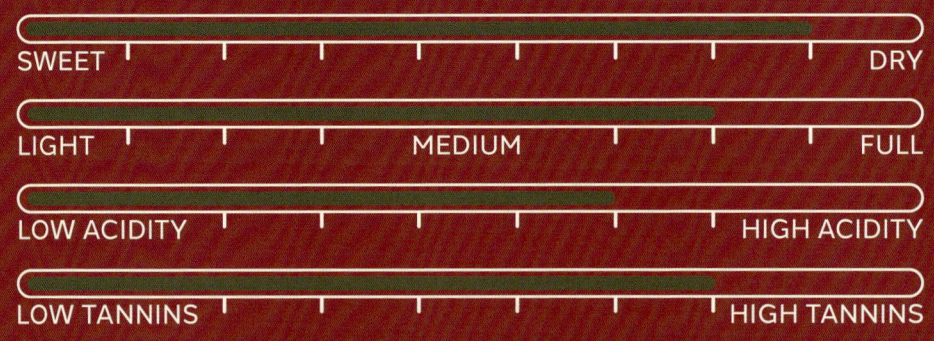

SWEET — DRY
LIGHT — MEDIUM — FULL
LOW ACIDITY — HIGH ACIDITY
LOW TANNINS — HIGH TANNINS

HANDLE:

 **SERVE** 60–68°F/ 15–20°C

 **GLASS TYPE** Standard Red

 **DECANT** 30-60 mins

  **CELLAR** 3-7 years

FAMOUS FOR:
ITS HERBACEOUS, RICH AND FRUIT-FORWARD BODY.

WE RECOMMEND:
Carobbio Chianti Classico 2017

GRAPES:
Sangiovese

REGION
Chianti DOCG, Italy

WINE STYLE:
Red

ALCOHOL CONTENT:
14%

PRICE:
£17-£19 | $28-$32

WHERE IT GROWS:

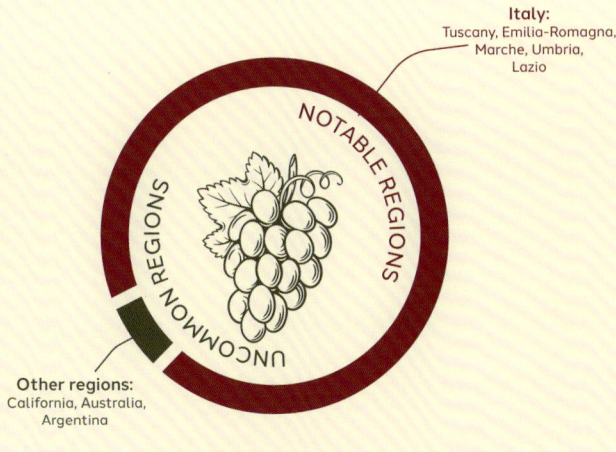

Italy: Tuscany, Emilia-Romagna, Marche, Umbria, Lazio

Other regions: California, Australia, Argentina

CINSAULT ROSÉ | BERRY SKIN ROSÉ
LANGUEDOC-ROUSSILLON, FRANCE

A light wine with fruit-forward aromas, this rosé is a perfect summer wine. With a mineral finish, this wine is both crisp and easy on the palate, making it a crowd-pleaser!

PRIMARY FLAVORS:

STRAWBERRY | RASPBERRY | POMEGRANATE | WHITE PEPPER | CHERRY

AROMAS:
Rose Petal, Orange Peel, Cherry, Strawberry, White Pepper.

FINISH:
Refreshing and lively.

PAIRS WELL WITH:
Salad, Garlic, Chicken.

TASTE PROFILE:

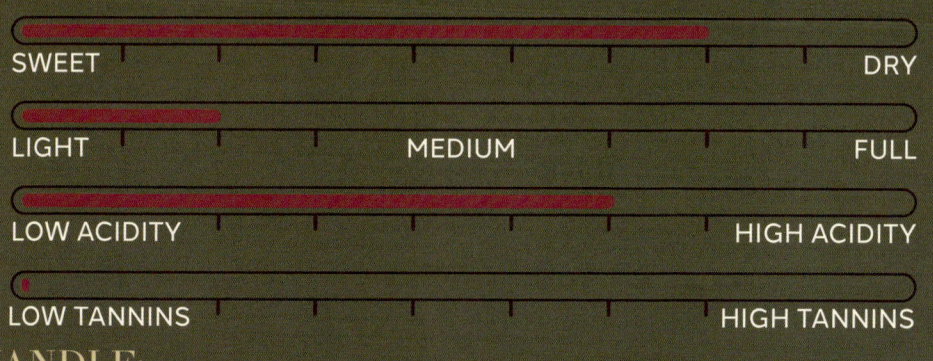

SWEET — DRY
LIGHT — MEDIUM — FULL
LOW ACIDITY — HIGH ACIDITY
LOW TANNINS — HIGH TANNINS

HANDLE:

SERVE
45-55°F/
7-12°C

GLASS TYPE
Universal

DECANT
No

CELLAR
No

FAMOUS FOR:
ITS QUALITY, VARIETAL EXPRESSION, ELEGANCE, AND VERSATILITY.

WE RECOMMEND:
Marques de Casa Concha Cinsault Rosé

GRAPES:
Cinsault, Garnacha

REGION:
Itata Valley, Chile

WINE STYLE:
Rosé

ALCOHOL CONTENT:
12.5%

PRICE:
£13-£17 | $20-$25

WHERE IT GROWS:

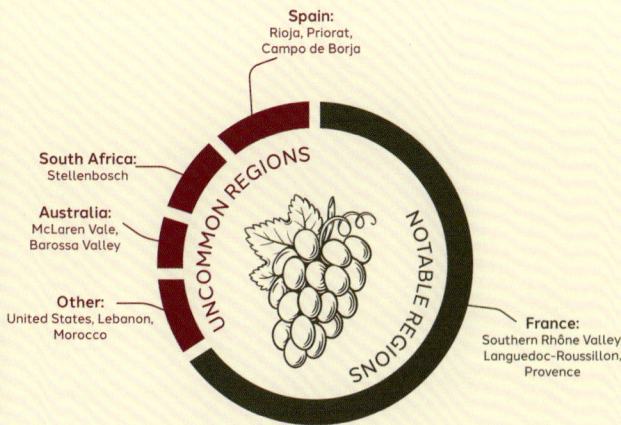

Spain: Rioja, Priorat, Campo de Borja

South Africa: Stellenbosch

Australia: McLaren Vale, Barossa Valley

Other: United States, Lebanon, Morocco

France: Southern Rhône Valley, Languedoc-Roussillon, Provence

COCOCCIOLA | BERRY SKIN WHITE
ABRUZZO, ITALY

Primarily grown in the Abruzzo region, in central Italy, Cococciola is a white grape wine characterized by its delicate citrus flavors and aromas, and is commonly found blended into other wines. On its own, it is zesty and fresh, making it a great summery wine!

PRIMARY FLAVORS:

LEMON — GRAPEFRUIT — LIME — APRICOT — GREEN APPLE

AROMAS:
Minerals, White Flower, Apricot, Lemon.

FINISH:
Zesty and crisp.

PAIRS WELL WITH:
Grilled Shrimp, Salads, Goat's Cheese.

TASTE PROFILE:

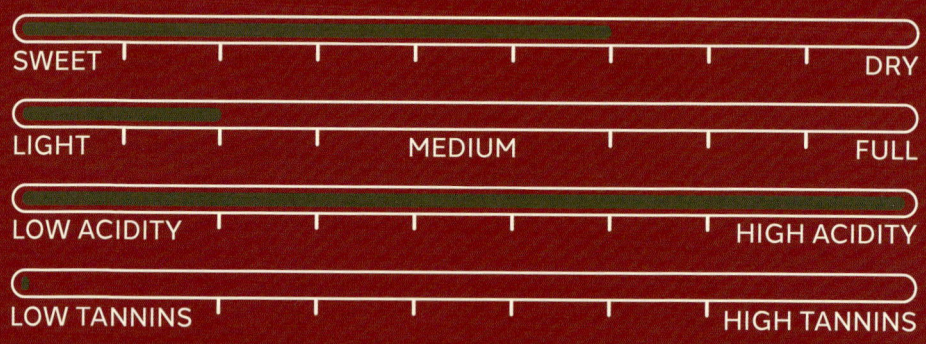

SWEET — DRY
LIGHT — MEDIUM — FULL
LOW ACIDITY — HIGH ACIDITY
LOW TANNINS — HIGH TANNINS

HANDLE:

 **SERVE** 45-50°F / 7-10°C

 **GLASS TYPE** Standard White

 **DECANT** No

 **CELLAR** 1-3 years

FAMOUS FOR:
ITS CITRUS-FORWARD FLAVOR PROFILE, AROMA, AND ZIPPY, MINERAL FINISH.

WE RECOMMEND:
Terre di Chieti IGT Cococciola 2023 Tenuta Ulisse

GRAPES:
Cococciola

REGION:
Abruzzo, Italy

WINE STYLE:
White

ALCOHOL CONTENT:
13%

PRICE:
£13-£16 | $15-$19

WHERE IT GROWS:

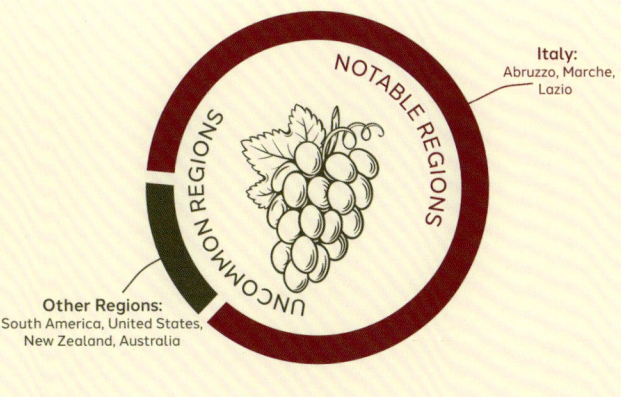

Italy: Abruzzo, Marche, Lazio

Other Regions: South America, United States, New Zealand, Australia

NOTABLE REGIONS / UNCOMMON REGIONS

DURAS | BERRY SKIN RED
TOULOUSE, FRANCE

Thought to be introduced to the French by the Romans over 2000 years ago, Duras is an ancient red known for its robust structure, fruity flavor and sometimes smoked aftertaste and aroma.

PRIMARY FLAVORS:

BLACKBERRY    **PLUM**   **BLACK PEPPER**   **TOBACCO**   **CHERRY**

AROMAS:
Dried Herbs, Smoke, Plum, Blackberry, Cherry.

FINISH:
Medium finish with fruit and spice.

PAIRS WELL WITH:
Ragu, Pork, Aged Cheese.

TASTE PROFILE:

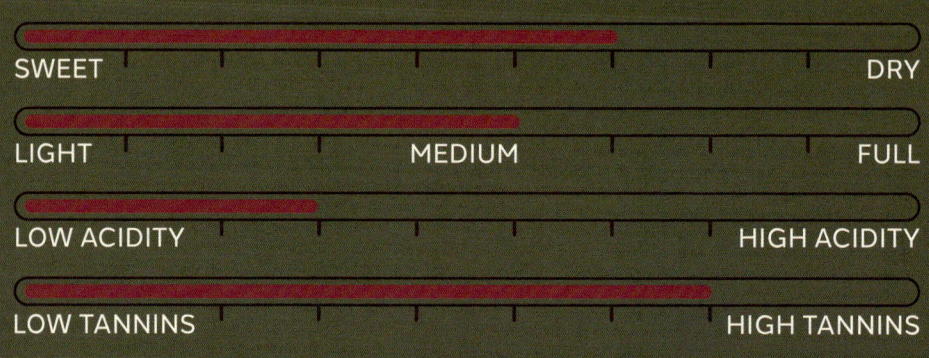

SWEET — DRY
LIGHT — MEDIUM — FULL
LOW ACIDITY — HIGH ACIDITY
LOW TANNINS — HIGH TANNINS

HANDLE:

 **SERVE** 60-65°F/ 15-18°C

 **GLASS TYPE** Standard Red

 **DECANT** 30-60 mins

 **CELLAR** 3-5 years

FAMOUS FOR:
ITS VELVETY TEXTURE AND ROUNDED BALANCE.

WE RECOMMEND:
Château L'Enclos des Rozes Le Petit Enclos, 2017

GRAPES:
Duras

REGION:
Gaillac, France

WINE STYLE:
Red

ALCOHOL CONTENT:
13.5%

PRICE:
£18-£22 | $18-$20

WHERE IT GROWS:

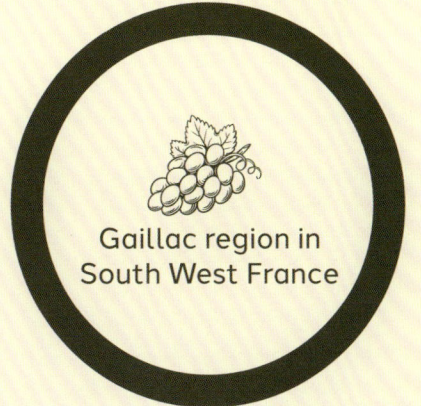

Gaillac region in South West France

There may be some experimental plantings of Duras. These regions could include parts of Europe, the United States, Australia, or South America.

TOP 5 MUST KNOW WINE REGIONS

RIOJA, SPAIN

Rioja's diverse terroir, quality wines, and rich cultural heritage make it a beloved wine region both in Spain and around the world.

GRAPE VARIETIES:
Rioja is known for its red wines made primarily from the Tempranillo grape variety. Other grape varieties used in Rioja wines include Garnacha (Grenache), Mazuelo (Carignan), and Graciano for red wines, and Viura and Malvasia for white wines.

MOST PRESTIGIOUS WINES:
Barolo and Barbaresco are often referred to as the "kings" of Italian wine. They are characterized by their complexity, aging potential, and distinctive flavors of cherry, roses, and tar. Barolo is known for its powerful structure and longevity, while Barbaresco is often described as more elegant and approachable in its youth.

KEY WINE REGIONS:
Rioja is divided into three subregions, each with its own distinct terroir and winemaking traditions: Rioja Alta, Rioja Alavesa and Rioja Oriental.

TERROIR:
Rioja's terroir combines climatic, geological, and viticultural factors to produce wines that are renowned for their elegance, complexity, and ageability.

FOOD PAIRING:
Rioja wines pair well with a variety of Spanish dishes, including roasted meats, grilled vegetables, tapas, and cured meats such as chorizo and jamón ibérico. The region's cuisine is influenced by its rich cultural heritage and culinary traditions.

GAMAY | BERRY SKIN RED
BEAUJOLAIS, FRANCE

Fruity, light and juicy, Gamay is cherished around the world for its delicate floral aromas and fruity flavor. With little-to-no tannin structure, Gamay is easy to drink, pairs well with many foods, and makes a great option for a summer red wine!

PRIMARY FLAVORS:

    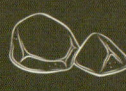

POMEGRANATE  | BLACKBERRY  | CHERRY | SOIL | WET STONE

AROMAS:
Violet, Cherry, Raspberry, Strawberry, Banana.

FINISH:
Crisp and lively.

PAIRS WELL WITH:
Roast Chicken, Grilled Fish.

TASTE PROFILE:

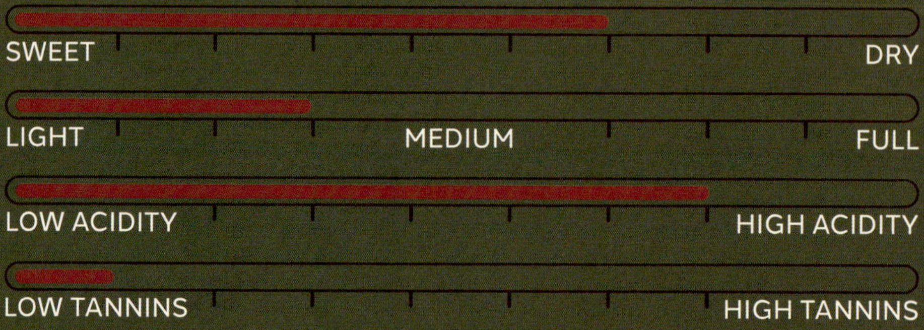

SWEET ———————————————————— DRY

LIGHT ———— MEDIUM ———— FULL

LOW ACIDITY ———————————————— HIGH ACIDITY

LOW TANNINS ———————————————— HIGH TANNINS

HANDLE:

SERVE
55-60°F/
14-15°C

GLASS TYPE
Standard
Red

DECANT
30 mins

CELLAR
3-7 years

FAMOUS FOR:
BEING LIGHT, CRISP, JUICY, AND VERSATILE.

WE RECOMMEND:
Domaine de la Jobeline Mâcon-Verzé Gamay 2018

GRAPES:
Gamay

REGION:
Burgundy, France

WINE STYLE:
Red

ALCOHOL CONTENT:
13%

PRICE:
£12-£16 | $16-$19

WHERE IT GROWS:

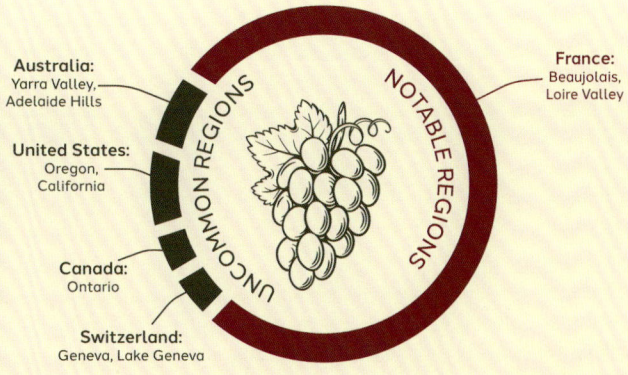

Australia: Yarra Valley, Adelaide Hills

United States: Oregon, California

Canada: Ontario

Switzerland: Geneva, Lake Geneva

France: Beaujolais, Loire Valley

UNCOMMON REGIONS | NOTABLE REGIONS

GRENACHE ROSÉ | BERRY SKIN ROSÉ
RHÔNE VALLEY, FRANCE

An easy-to-drink option that is deep in color, Grenache Rosé is a deliciously floral and juicy option but with a surprisingly dry finish. This makes it a great summery wine that pairs well with a range of foods, or can be drunk on its own!

PRIMARY FLAVORS:

STRAWBERRY   RASPBERRY   LEMON   CHERRY   PEACH

AROMAS:
Strawberry, Raspberry, Orange Flower, Rose, Stone.

FINISH:
Refreshing and crisp.

PAIRS WELL WITH:
Chicken, Seafood, Pasta.

TASTE PROFILE:

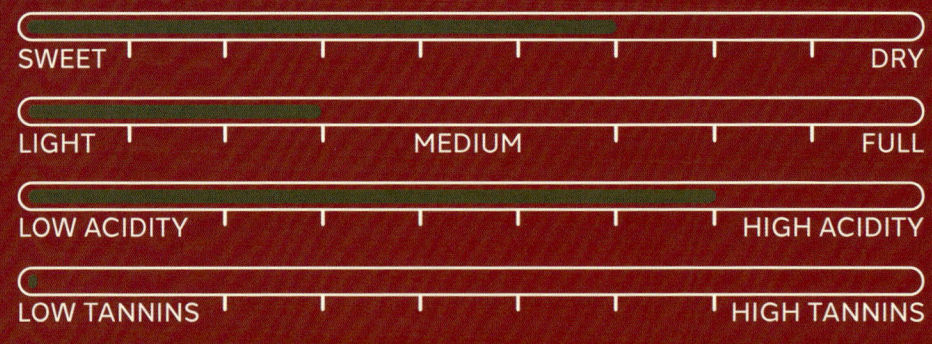

SWEET — DRY
LIGHT — MEDIUM — FULL
LOW ACIDITY — HIGH ACIDITY
LOW TANNINS — HIGH TANNINS

HANDLE:

SERVE
45-55°F/
7-13°C

GLASS TYPE
Standard White

DECANT
No

CELLAR
1-3 years

FAMOUS FOR:
ITS SWEET YET DRY ROSÉ WITH JUICY FLAVORS AND A CRISP AFTERTASTE.

WE RECOMMEND:
Languedoc DOP Côte des Roses Rosé 2022 Gérard Bertrand

GRAPES:
Cinsault, Grenache, Syrah

REGION:
Languedoc-Roussillon, France

WINE STYLE:
Rosé

ALCOHOL CONTENT:
13%

PRICE:
£8-£11 | $14-$17

WHERE IT GROWS:

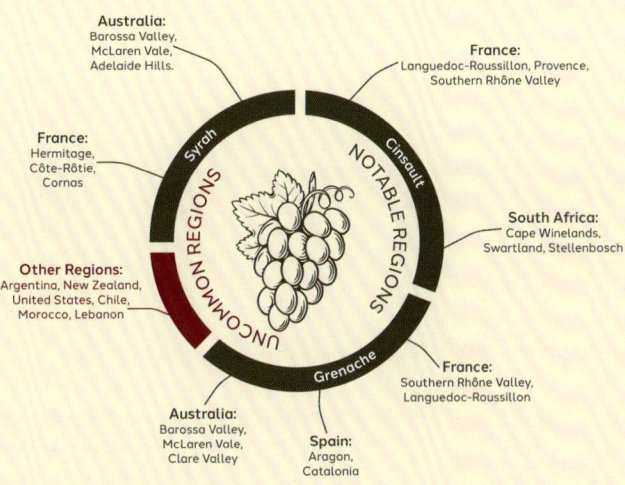

GRENACHE | BERRY SKIN RED
RHÔNE VALLEY, FRANCE

Known as Garnacha in Spanish, Grenache is a full bodied, low tannin red wine with fruity flavors and an earthy, spicy tang. Originally from Spain, this grape is now extremely popular in France, particularly in the Southern Rhône Valley!

PRIMARY FLAVORS:

   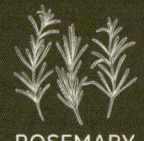 

CLOVE — PLUM — CHERRY — ROSEMARY — BLACK PEPPER

AROMAS:
Cinnamon, Black Pepper, Cherry, Raspberry, Violet.

FINISH:
Long and fruity.

PAIRS WELL WITH:
Grilled Meats, Pasta, Roasted Vegetables.

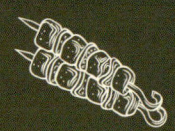

TASTE PROFILE:

SWEET ——————————————●———— DRY

LIGHT ——————●——————————— FULL (MEDIUM)

LOW ACIDITY ——————————●———— HIGH ACIDITY

LOW TANNINS ——●————————————— HIGH TANNINS

HANDLE:

 **SERVE** 60-65°F / 15-18°C

 **GLASS TYPE** Standard Red

 **DECANT** 30 mins

 **CELLAR** 5-10 years

FAMOUS FOR:
ITS BRIGHT COLOR AS WELL AS ITS FRUITY, EARTHY NOTES.

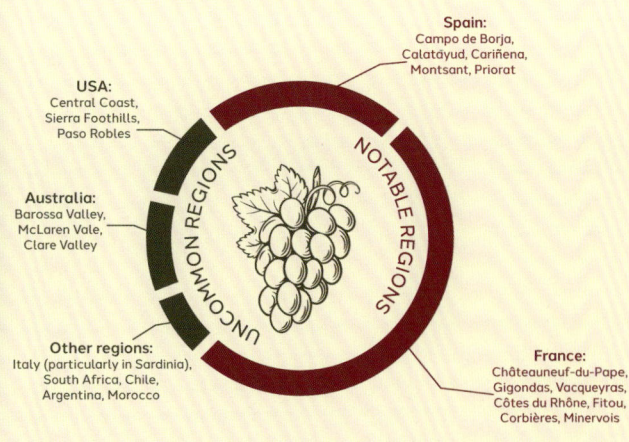

WE RECOMMEND:
Mas de L'Auris Côtes du Roussillon Rouge, 2022

GRAPES:
Grenache Noir

REGION:
Côtes du Roussillon, France

WINE STYLE:
Red

ALCOHOL CONTENT:
13.5%

PRICE:
£11-£15 | $15-$18

WHERE IT GROWS:

Spain: Campo de Borja, Calatayud, Cariñena, Montsant, Priorat

USA: Central Coast, Sierra Foothills, Paso Robles

Australia: Barossa Valley, McLaren Vale, Clare Valley

Other regions: Italy (particularly in Sardinia), South Africa, Chile, Argentina, Morocco

France: Châteauneuf-du-Pape, Gigondas, Vacqueyras, Côtes du Rhône, Fitou, Corbières, Minervois

NOTABLE REGIONS / UNCOMMON REGIONS

- 35 -

TAKE A CLOSER LOOK

Oh, look - a new glass of wine! Full and ready for drinking – but before you take that first sip, let's decode the subtle language of its appearance, and what it can tell us about the flavor.

COLOR
The color of wine can vary widely, offering clues about its age, grape variety, and winemaking techniques. Reds can range from pale ruby to deep garnet, while whites can span from pale straw to golden yellow. Rosé wines typically exhibit shades of pink.

VISCOSITY
Swirling the wine in the glass reveals its viscosity, or "legs". Thicker, slower-moving legs may suggest higher alcohol content or more residual sugar, indicating a fuller-bodied wine.

EFFERVESCENCE
In sparkling wines, observing the size and persistence of bubbles can indicate its quality and production method. Finer bubbles that rise steadily are often associated with higher quality sparkling wines.

CLARITY
Clear, bright wines are often considered youthful and well-made, while cloudy or hazy appearances might suggest a less filtered or older wine.

BRILLIANCE
A wine's brilliance refers to its overall shine and sparkle. Bright, vibrant wines are often associated with freshness and quality, while dull or muted appearances might suggest oxidation or aging.

RIM VARIATION
Tipping the glass slightly and observing the wine's color at the edge, or "rim", can provide insights into its age. Wines with a clear distinction between the center and rim may indicate maturity and aging potential.

Love
LIKE WINE
GETS BETTER
WITH
Time

LAMBRUSCO | BERRY SKIN RED
EMILIA-ROMAGNA, ITALY

This sparkling red is a great refreshing option for those who love bubbles, but want a taste that carries a little more body and flavor. Usually Italian made, this wine is a crisp and chilled option that carries light and juicy berry notes.

PRIMARY FLAVORS:

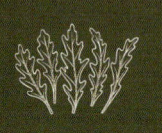

PLUM | BLACKBERRY | DRIED HERBS | CHERRY | SOIL

AROMAS:
Strawberry, Cherry, Dried Herbs, Hibiscus, Orange Blossom.

FINISH:
Lively and refreshing.

PAIRS WELL WITH:
Prosciutto, Parmigiano-Reggiano, Pasta.

TASTE PROFILE:

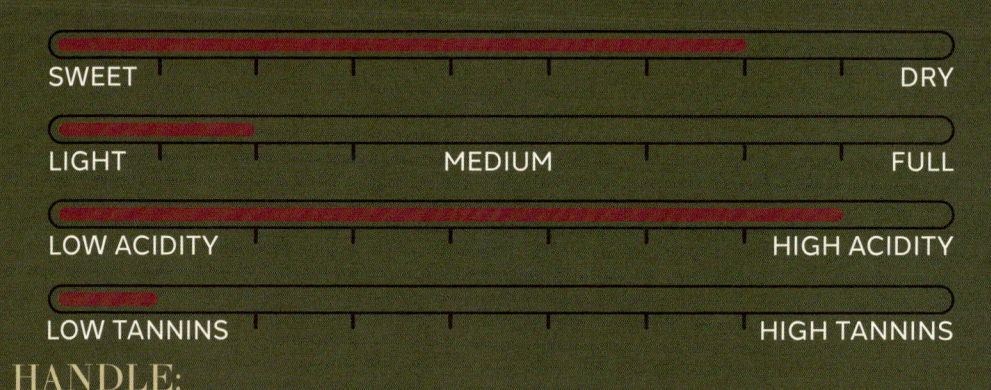

SWEET —————————————————— DRY

LIGHT —————— MEDIUM —————— FULL

LOW ACIDITY —————————————— HIGH ACIDITY

LOW TANNINS —————————————— HIGH TANNINS

HANDLE:

SERVE
46-50°F/
8-10°C

GLASS TYPE
Tulip

DECANT
No

CELLAR
No

FAMOUS FOR:
ITS RUBY-RED COLOR AND LIVELY, CRISP FIZZ.

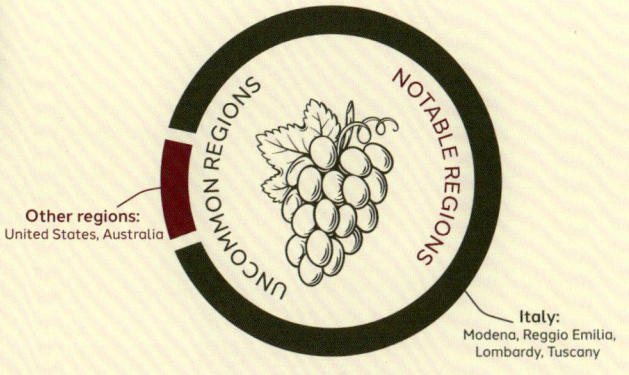

WE RECOMMEND:
Medici Ermete Concerto Lambrusco Reggiano 2022

GRAPES:
Lambrusco Salamino

REGION:
Emilia-Romagna, Italy

WINE STYLE:
Sparkling Red

ALCOHOL CONTENT:
11.5%

PRICE:
£9-£14 | $20-$25

WHERE IT GROWS:

Other regions: United States, Australia

Italy: Modena, Reggio Emilia, Lombardy, Tuscany

UNCOMMON REGIONS | NOTABLE REGIONS

MADEIRA | WINE TYPE: FORTIFIED WINE

MADEIRA, PORTUGAL

Produced on the Portuguese island of Madeira, this sweet fortified wine is famous for its complex, caramel flavor. Ranging in styles from dry to sweet, this wine generally has signature characteristics that set it apart from other fortified wines.

PRIMARY FLAVORS:

| CARAMEL | TOFFEE | NUTS | CITRUS PEEL | RAISINS |

AROMAS:
Caramel, Apple, Burnt Sugar, Cinnamon, Hazelnut.

FINISH:
Long and sweet.

PAIRS WELL WITH:
Cheese, Nuts, Chocolate.

TASTE PROFILE:

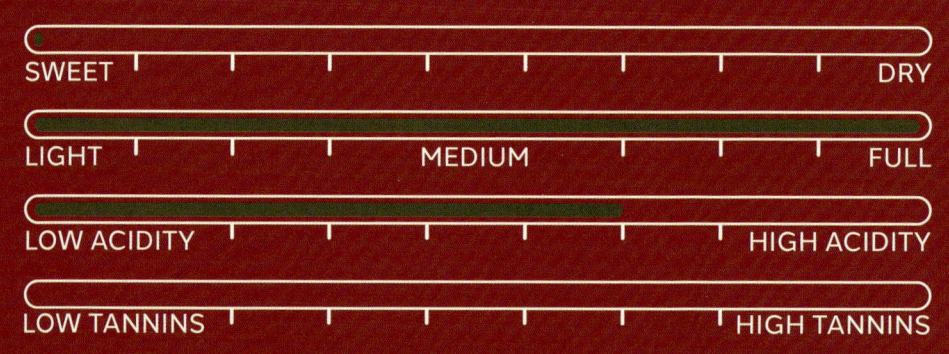

SWEET |—————————————————————————————| DRY

LIGHT |—————————————————————————————| FULL

LOW ACIDITY |—————————————————————————————| HIGH ACIDITY

LOW TANNINS |—————————————————————————————| HIGH TANNINS

HANDLE:

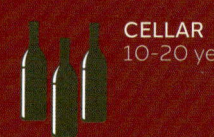

SERVE
55–60°F/
12–15°C

GLASS TYPE
Sweet Wine

DECANT
No

CELLAR
10-20 years

FAMOUS FOR:
ITS EARTHY EDGE AND CARAMEL, NUTTY FLAVORS.

WE RECOMMEND:
Blandy's Anos 5 Years Reserva Rich Madeira N.V.

GRAPES:
Bual & Malmsey

REGION:
Madeira, Portugal

WINE STYLE:
Fortified

ALCOHOL CONTENT:
19%

PRICE:
£15-£19 | $18-$23

WHERE IT GROWS:

Bual and Malmsey are both varieties of Madeira wine grapes, primarily grown on the Portuguese island of Madeira.

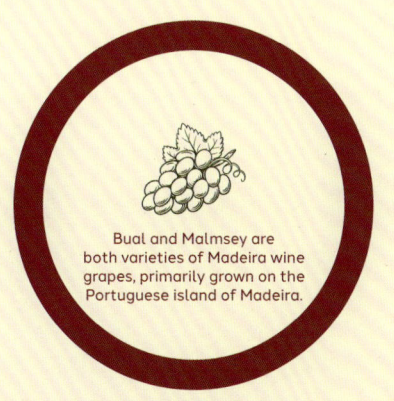

In regions with a focus on fortified or dessert wines, there may be some interest in experimenting with Bual and Malmsey grapes. However, such plantings are likely to be limited and are primarily driven by niche or experimental winemaking projects.

MOSCATO D'ASTI | BERRY SKIN WHITE
PIEDMONT, ITALY

Typically a sweet or semi-sweet white wine, Moscato d'Asti is a type of Moscato that is semi-sparkling. These are aromatic and sweet, but also have a zippy acidity and clean finish, making it a delicious summery sipper!

PRIMARY FLAVORS:

LEMON ORANGE PEAR PEACH ORANGE BLOSSOM

AROMAS:
Grape, Honeysuckle, Peach, Stone, Jasmine.

FINISH:
Refreshing and bright.

PAIRS WELL WITH:
Curry, Chili, Light Cake.

TASTE PROFILE:

SWEET — DRY
LIGHT — MEDIUM — FULL
LOW ACIDITY — HIGH ACIDITY
LOW TANNINS — HIGH TANNINS

HANDLE:

SERVE
45-50°F/
7-10°C

GLASS TYPE
Standard White

DECANT
No

CELLAR
No

FAMOUS FOR:
ITS STONE FRUIT TASTE AND FLORAL AROMA.

WE RECOMMEND:
Cantine Povero Campo del Palio Moscato d'Asti 2015

GRAPES:
Moscato

REGION:
Piedmont, Italy

WINE STYLE:
White

ALCOHOL CONTENT:
5.5%

PRICE:
£10-£14 | $10-$14

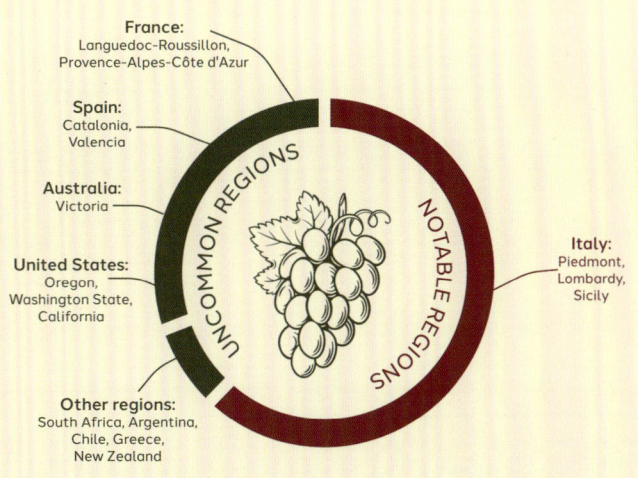

WHERE IT GROWS:

France:
Languedoc-Roussillon, Provence-Alpes-Côte d'Azur

Spain:
Catalonia, Valencia

Australia:
Victoria

United States:
Oregon, Washington State, California

Other regions:
South Africa, Argentina, Chile, Greece, New Zealand

Italy:
Piedmont, Lombardy, Sicily

UNCOMMON REGIONS | NOTABLE REGIONS

THE NOSE KNOWS
SMELL LIKE A SOMMELIER

Next we'll dive into the fascinating world of wine aromas. Becoming skilled at identifying wine aromas can heighten your tasting experience and impress your friends and guests.

PRACTICE REGULARLY:
- Make a habit of smelling a wide variety of items daily. This includes food, flowers, spices, and even non-food items like wood or leather.
- Regularly taste and smell different types of wine. Focus on identifying primary aromas (fruit, floral), secondary aromas (such as yeast), and tertiary aromas (oak or earthy notes).

BUILD A SCENT VOCABULARY:
- Document the smells you encounter, describing them in detail.
- Learn and use common wine descriptors like fruity, floral, spicy, earthy, woody, etc.

ENGAGE WITH OTHER SENSES:
- When tasting wine, pay attention to how taste and smell interact. Notice how the aroma complements the flavor.
- Observe the color and clarity of the wine, which can offer clues about its characteristics and potential aromas.

USE TOOLS AND KITS:
- Invest in a wine aroma kit, which contains vials of common wine scents.
- Practice blind tasting with friends. It challenges your nose to identify aromas without visual cues.

HEALTHY LIFESTYLE:
- Reduce exposure to strong perfumes, scented candles, and other overpowering scents that can desensitize your nose.
- A well-hydrated body and a healthy diet can improve your overall sense of smell.

MINDFUL SMELLING:
- When you smell wine, do so mindfully. Swirl the wine in the glass, take a deep inhale, and think about the aromas you detect.
- Smell different wines side by side to note the differences and similarities in their aromas.

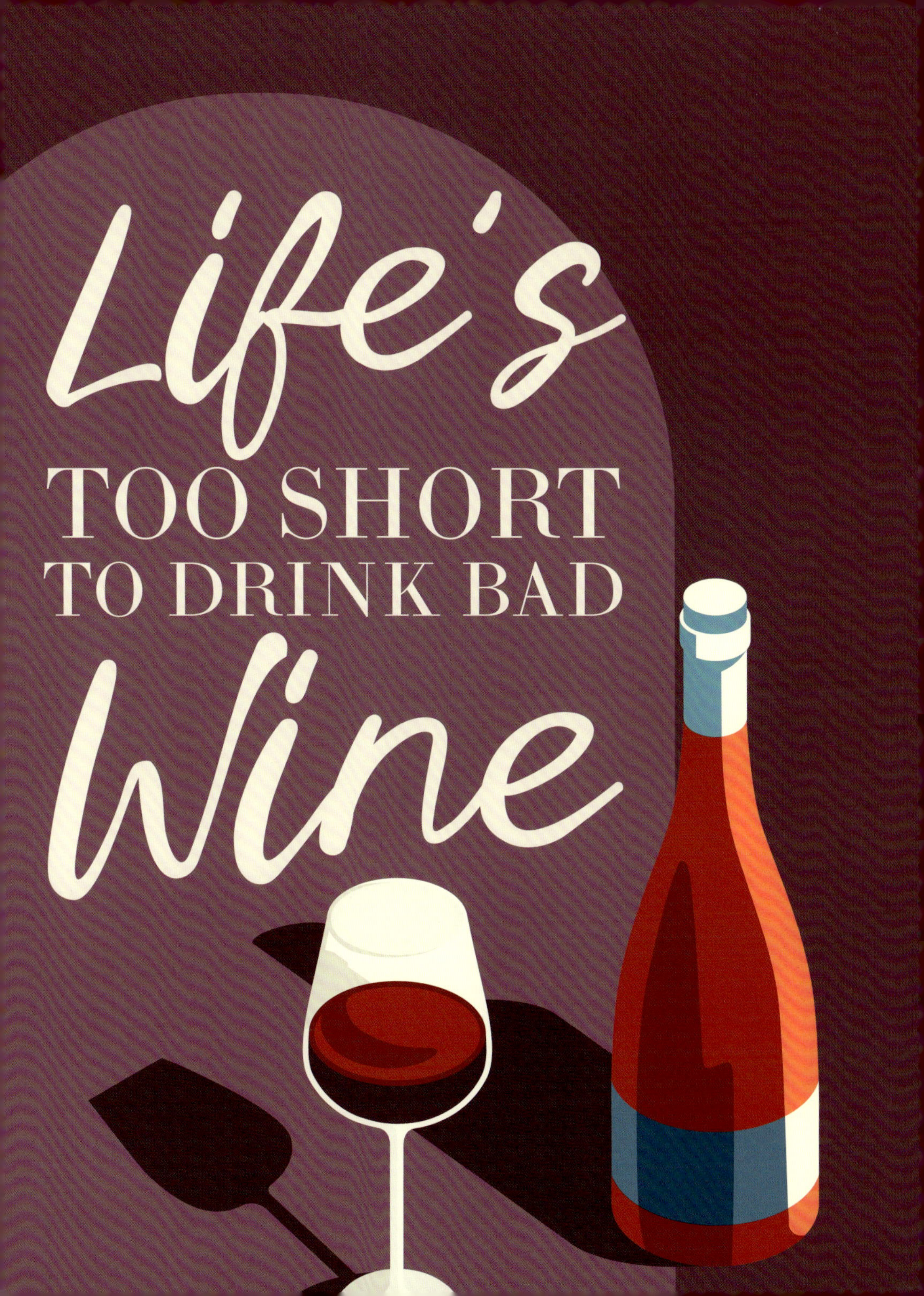
Life's
TOO SHORT
TO DRINK BAD
Wine

NEBBIOLO | BERRY SKIN RED
BAROLO, ITALY

One of Italy's most important red wines, Nebbiolo is traditionally found in the Barolo region, where wines are characterized by their dainty aromas and strong tannins that create a memorable and bold red with an acidic, fresh finish.

PRIMARY FLAVORS:

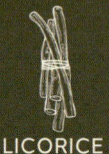

CHERRY | ROSE | LICORICE | TOBACCO | HERBS

AROMAS:
Cherry, Raspberry, Rose, Truffle, Leather.

FINISH:
Long, fruity, and savory.

PAIRS WELL WITH:
Truffle, Cream Cheese, Roast Lamb.

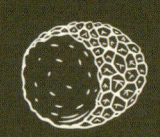

TASTE PROFILE:

SWEET —————————————————— DRY

LIGHT ——————— MEDIUM ——————— FULL

LOW ACIDITY —————————————————— HIGH ACIDITY

LOW TANNINS —————————————————— HIGH TANNINS

HANDLE:

SERVE
60-65°F/
15-18°C

GLASS TYPE
Burgundy

DECANT
1 hr

CELLAR
5-10 years

FAMOUS FOR:
ITS INTENSE TANNINS AND EARTHY AROMA.

WE RECOMMEND:
Cascina Vengore Belgardo Terre Alfieri Nebbiolo

GRAPES:
Nebbiolo

REGION:
Piedmont, Italy

WINE STYLE:
Red

ALCOHOL CONTENT:
14%

PRICE:
£21-£24 | $19-$24

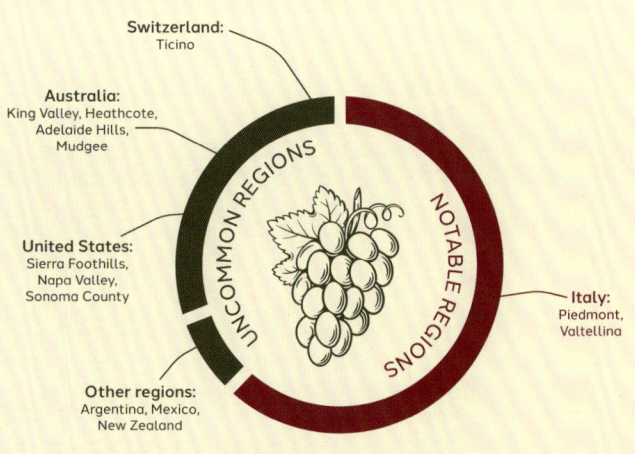

WHERE IT GROWS:

Switzerland: Ticino

Australia: King Valley, Heathcote, Adelaide Hills, Mudgee

United States: Sierra Foothills, Napa Valley, Sonoma County

Other regions: Argentina, Mexico, New Zealand

Italy: Piedmont, Valtellina

UNCOMMON REGIONS | NOTABLE REGIONS

SAUVIGNON BLANC (NZ) | BERRY SKI WHITE
AWATERE VALLEY, NEW ZEALAND

Unlike French Sauvignon Blanc, that is known for its minerality and delicate flavor, New Zealand Sauvignon Blanc is much more aromatic and intense, sharing the zingy acidity but with more tropical fruit notes.

PRIMARY FLAVORS:

PEAR · LEMON · MANGO · APPLE · GREEN PEPPER

AROMAS:
Passionfruit, Grapefruit, Gooseberry, Pineapple, Kiwi.

FINISH:
Lingering and crisp.

PAIRS WELL WITH:
Shellfish, Goat's Cheese, Pasta.

TASTE PROFILE:

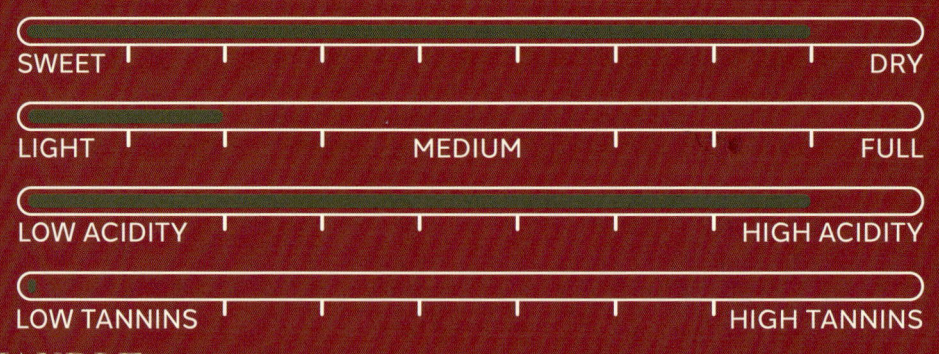

SWEET —————————————————— DRY
LIGHT —————————————————— FULL
LOW ACIDITY —————————————————— HIGH ACIDITY
LOW TANNINS —————————————————— HIGH TANNINS

HANDLE:

SERVE
45-55°F/
7-13°C

GLASS TYPE
Standard White

DECANT
No

CELLAR
3-5 years

FAMOUS FOR:
RICH BODY, DEEP COLOR, AND COMPLEX DRY FRUITINESS.

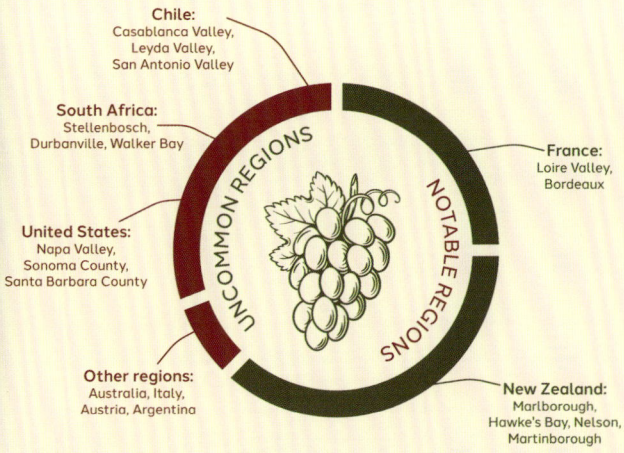

WE RECOMMEND:
Yealands Single Vineyard Sauvignon Blanc 2022

GRAPES:
Sauvignon Blanc

REGION:
Awatere Valley, New Zealand

WINE STYLE:
White

ALCOHOL CONTENT:
12.5%

PRICE:
£13–£15 | $14–$16

WHERE IT GROWS:

Chile: Casablanca Valley, Leyda Valley, San Antonio Valley

South Africa: Stellenbosch, Durbanville, Walker Bay

United States: Napa Valley, Sonoma County, Santa Barbara County

Other regions: Australia, Italy, Austria, Argentina

France: Loire Valley, Bordeaux

New Zealand: Marlborough, Hawke's Bay, Nelson, Martinborough

UNCOMMON REGIONS | NOTABLE REGIONS

ORANGE WINE | WINE TYPE: ORANGE
KAKHETI, GEORGIA

Orange wine is a skin-contact white grape wine that is generally orange in hue, due to the skins being left on the grapes during fermentation. Whilst grape variety and aging all play a part in the wine's flavor and aroma, most orange wines have some crucial similarities that set them apart from white wines!

PRIMARY FLAVORS:

| PEACH | APRICOT | PINEAPPLE | ORANGE BLOSSOM | HONEY |

AROMAS:
Peach, Honeysuckle, Hazelnut, Dried Zest, Grapefruit.

FINISH:
Long and textural.

PAIRS WELL WITH:
Lamb, Hard Cheese, Eggplant (Aubergine).

TASTE PROFILE:

SWEET —————————————————— DRY (towards dry)

LIGHT —————— MEDIUM —————— FULL (medium)

LOW ACIDITY —————————————— HIGH ACIDITY (high)

LOW TANNINS —————————————— HIGH TANNINS (high)

HANDLE:

SERVE
50-57°F/
10-14°C

GLASS TYPE
Standard
Red

DECANT
15-30 mins

CELLAR
5-7 years

- 50 -

FAMOUS FOR:
ITS HIGH TANNINS, FULL BODY, AND CRISP, ZESTY TASTE.

WE RECOMMEND:
Herdade do Rocim Amphora Branco 2020

GRAPES:
Perrum, Rabo de Ovelha and Manteúdo

REGION:
Alentejo, Portugal

WINE STYLE:
Orange

ALCOHOL CONTENT:
13%

PRICE:
£20-£25 | $20-$25

WHERE IT GROWS:

Perum, Rabo de Ovelha, and Manteúdo are indigenous grape varieties primarily associated with Portugal, particularly in the wine regions of the Alentejo and Algarve.

These grape varieties may also be found in other wine regions of Portugal, particularly in areas where winemakers prioritize traditional and indigenous grape varieties.

FOOD PAIRNG

Food pairing is a highly subjective topic and depends on personal tastes, but here are some ways to find great and (hopefully) fail-safe pairings!

COMPLEMENTARY PAIRINGS:

Chardonnay:
- SOFT CHEESE
- ROAST CHICKEN
- LOBSTER

Sauvignon Blanc:
- GOAT'S CHEESE
- GRILLED VEGETABLES
- OYSTERS

Pinot Grigio:
- CHICKEN
- SEAFOOD
- SOFT CHEESES

Riesling:
- PORK TENDERLOIN
- SHRIMP
- BLUE CHEESE

Cabernet Sauvignon:
- GOUDA
- LAMB CHOPS
- STEAK

Syrah/Shiraz:
- DUCK
- AGED CHEESE
- BARBECUE RIBS

Malbec:
- LAMB
- BARBECUE RIBS
- BLUE CHEESE

Pinot Noir:
- STEAK
- ROAST CHICKEN
- GRILLED SALMON

Creative pairings demonstrate how thinking outside the box can lead to delicious and memorable flavor combinations. Don't be afraid to experiment with different wines and cuisines to discover your own unique pairings!

CREATIVE PAIRINGS:

Chardonnay:
- VEGETABLE SKEWERS
- SASHIMI
- APPLE PIE

Sauvignon Blanc:
- SUSHI
- SHRIMP SKEWERS
- FETA CHEESE

Pinot Grigio:
- VEGETABLE STIR-FRY
- SUSHI
- CHILI CON CARNE

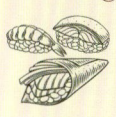

Riesling:
- CHEESECAKE
- SUSHI
- FISH TACOS

Cabernet Sauvignon:
- GOURMET BURGERS
- SALMON
- GRILLED VEGETABLES

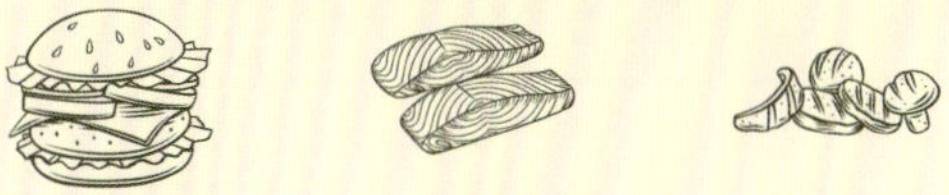

Syrah/Shiraz:
- PIZZA
- MOLE POBLANO
- DARK CHOCOLATE

Malbec:
- SPICY CHILI
- MUSHROOM RAVIOLI
- DARK CHOCOLATE

Pinot Noir:
- DUCK
- BEET SALAD
- VEGETABLE STIR-FRY

PÉTILLANT NATUREL | BERRY SKIN WHITE

LOIRE VALLEY, FRANCE

Essentially natural sparkling wine, the fermentation of Pet Nat is completed in the bottle, resulting in a natural carbonation and mostly cloudy finish. This has varied results in the wine, but these are generally connected with similarities exclusive to this style of winemaking.

PRIMARY FLAVORS:

LEMON | APPLE | PEAR | PEACH | HONEYSUCKLE

AROMAS:
Jasmine, Orange Blossom, Almond, Brioche, Apple.

FINISH:
Crisp and refreshing.

PAIRS WELL WITH:
Soft Cheese, Salted Popcorn, Sushi.

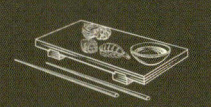

TASTE PROFILE:

SWEET |———————————————————| DRY

LIGHT |———————————————————| FULL

LOW ACIDITY |———————————————————| HIGH ACIDITY

LOW TANNINS |———————————————————| HIGH TANNINS

HANDLE:

SERVE
45-55°F/
7-13°C

GLASS TYPE
Tulip

DECANT
No

CELLAR
No

FAMOUS FOR:
ITS CLOUDY FINISH AND LIVELY, TART TASTE.

WE RECOMMEND:
Chateau tour des gendres pet nat

GRAPES:
Chenin Blanc, Sauvignon Blanc

REGION:
Bergerac, France

WINE STYLE:
Sparkling

ALCOHOL CONTENT:
12.5%

PRICE:
£17-£21 | $23-$27

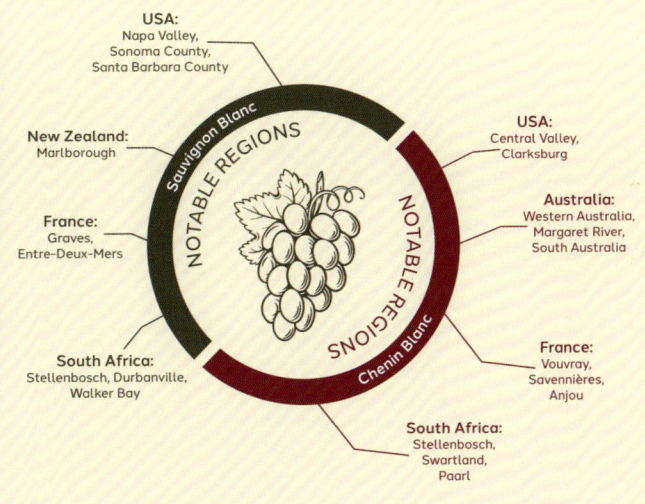

WHERE IT GROWS:

Sauvignon Blanc — NOTABLE REGIONS

- **USA:** Napa Valley, Sonoma County, Santa Barbara County
- **New Zealand:** Marlborough
- **France:** Graves, Entre-Deux-Mers
- **South Africa:** Stellenbosch, Durbanville, Walker Bay

Chenin Blanc — NOTABLE REGIONS

- **USA:** Central Valley, Clarksburg
- **Australia:** Western Australia, Margaret River, South Australia
- **France:** Vouvray, Savennières, Anjou
- **South Africa:** Stellenbosch, Swartland, Paarl

PINOTAGE | BERRY SKIN RED
CONSTANTIA (CT), SOUTH AFRICA

A combination of Cinsaut and Pinot Noir, Pinotage is a predominantly South African grown red grape, producing wine that is dense in color and bold in flavor – a great alternative to Shiraz.

PRIMARY FLAVORS:

| PLUM | RASPBERRY | TOBACCO | RED PEPPER | SOIL |

AROMAS:
Plum, Cherry, Smoke, Violet, Leather.

FINISH:
Medium to long, with lingering fruit flavors.

PAIRS WELL WITH:
Hearty Stews, Lamb, Goat's Cheese.

TASTE PROFILE:

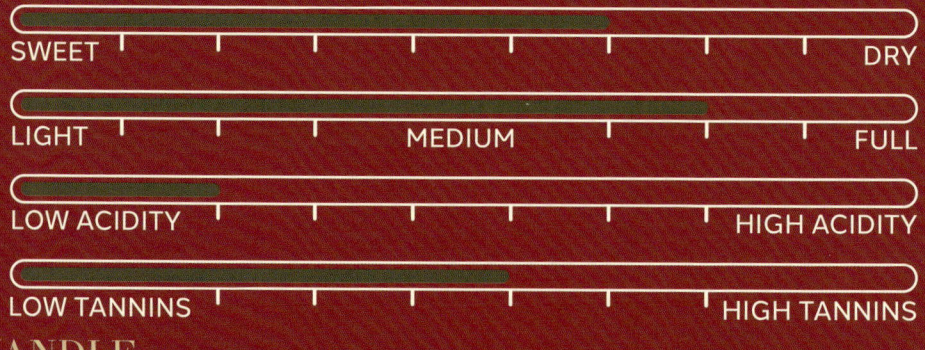

SWEET ————————————————— DRY (towards dry)

LIGHT ————————————————— FULL (towards full)

LOW ACIDITY ————————————————— HIGH ACIDITY (low)

LOW TANNINS ————————————————— HIGH TANNINS (medium)

HANDLE:

SERVE
61-64°F /
16-18°C

GLASS TYPE
Burgundy

DECANT
30-60 mins

CELLAR
5-10 years

- 56 -

FAMOUS FOR:
ITS INKY HUE AND COMPLEX FRUIT FLAVORS, WITH A SAVORY FINISH.

WE RECOMMEND:
Painted Wolf Guillermo Pinotage 2020

GRAPES:
Pinotage

REGION:
Paarl, South Africa

WINE STYLE:
Red

ALCOHOL CONTENT:
13.5%

PRICE:
£16-£20 | $21-$24

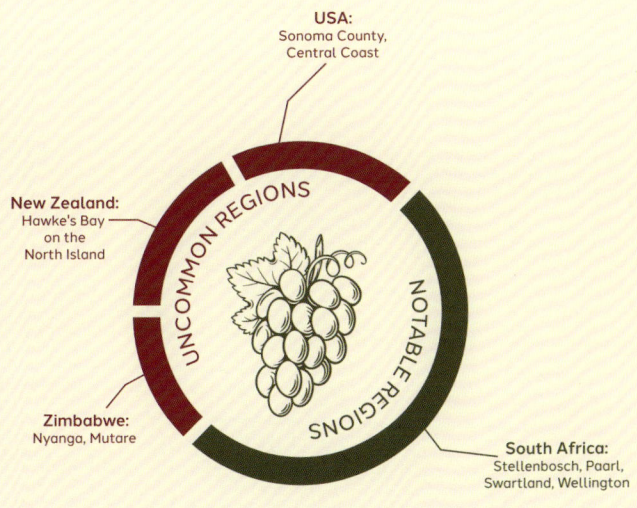

WHERE IT GROWS:

USA: Sonoma County, Central Coast

New Zealand: Hawke's Bay on the North Island

Zimbabwe: Nyanga, Mutare

South Africa: Stellenbosch, Paarl, Swartland, Wellington

UNCOMMON REGIONS | NOTABLE REGIONS

PLAVAC MALI | BERRY SKIN ROSE
DALMATIA, CROATIA

A relatively unknown red wine native to Croatia, Plavac Mali is a great alternative to more mainstream wines such as Primitivo, and provides a deep color and herbaceous taste, with a crisp and fresh minerality to them!

PRIMARY FLAVORS:

- BLACKBERRY
- PLUM 
- THYME 
- ROSEMARY 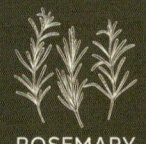
- CINNAMON 

AROMAS:
Blackberry, Plum, Violet, Black Pepper, Vanilla.

FINISH:
Long, fruity and savory.

PAIRS WELL WITH:
Lamb Chops, Stews, Beef.

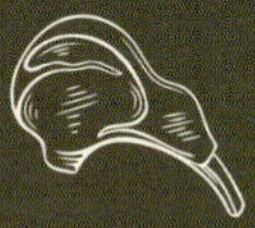

TASTE PROFILE:

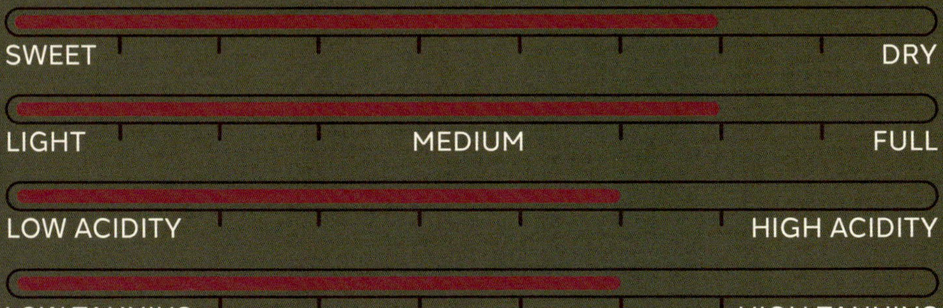

SWEET —————————————— DRY (toward dry)

LIGHT —————————————— FULL (medium)

LOW ACIDITY —————————————— HIGH ACIDITY (medium-high)

LOW TANNINS —————————————— HIGH TANNINS (medium-high)

HANDLE:

- **SERVE**: 60-64°F / 16-18°C
- **GLASS TYPE**: Burgundy 
- **DECANT**: 30 mins 
- **CELLAR**: 3-8 years

FAMOUS FOR:
ITS RICH AND EARTHY SPICE WITH JUICY HITS.

WE RECOMMEND:
Dingač 2019, Matusko

GRAPES:
Plavac Mali

REGION:
Dalmatia, Croatia

WINE STYLE:
Red

ALCOHOL CONTENT:
14.3%

PRICE:
£13-£17 | $13-$20

WHERE IT GROWS:

Plavac Mali is a red grape variety primarily associated with Croatia, particularly with the Dalmatian coast region.

Plavac Mali is well adapted to the rugged terrain and coastal vineyards of the Dalmatian coast, where it thrives in the region's limestone soils and benefits from the cooling influence of the Adriatic Sea. The grape is a key component in many traditional Croatian wines.

PROSECCO | BERRY SKIN WHITE

VENETO, ITALY

Italy's number 1 sparkling wine, Prosecco is savored by the world-over for its crisp apple flavors and lively carbonation! Versatile, aromatic, and light, Prosecco is an easy-drinker, and is also used in many cocktails due to its versatility and fresh elements.

PRIMARY FLAVORS:

APPLE · PEAR · HONEY · ALMOND · CREAM

AROMAS:
Peach, Pear, White Flower, Lemon, Honeysuckle.

FINISH:
Clean and refreshing.

PAIRS WELL WITH:
Light Cheese, Almonds, Pad Thai.

TASTE PROFILE:

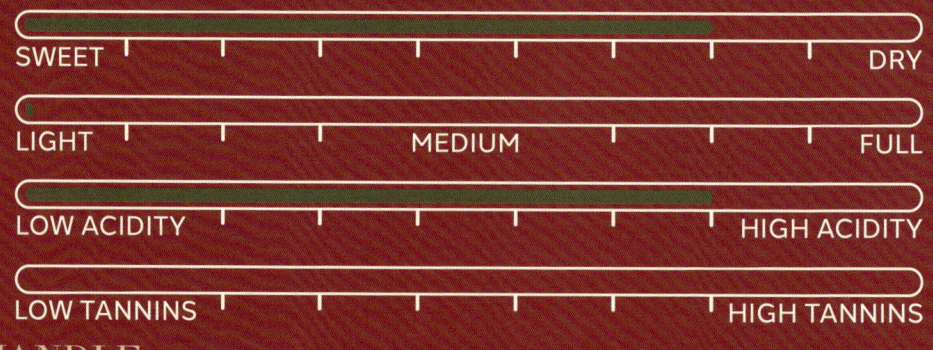

SWEET —————————————————————— DRY

LIGHT —————————————————————— FULL

LOW ACIDITY —————————————————————— HIGH ACIDITY

LOW TANNINS —————————————————————— HIGH TANNINS

HANDLE:

SERVE
38–45°F/
3–7°C

GLASS TYPE
Flute

DECANT
No

CELLAR
1–3 years

FAMOUS FOR:
BEING BRIGHT, CRISP, AND DELICIOUSLY REFRESHING.

WE RECOMMEND:
SalvaTerra Via Vai Prosecco

GRAPES:
Glera

REGION:
Veneto, Italy

WINE STYLE:
Sparkling

ALCOHOL CONTENT:
10.5%

PRICE:
£9-£14 | $13-$17

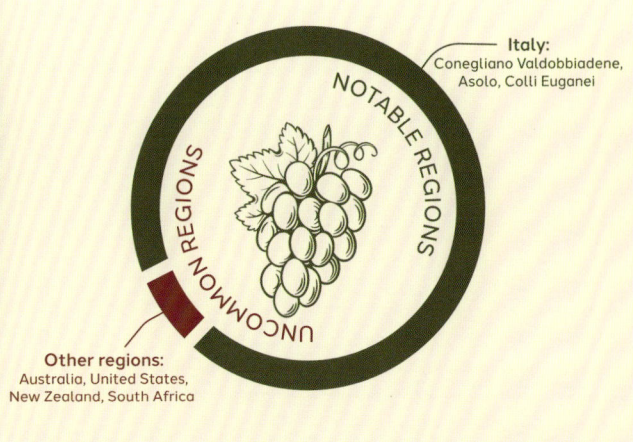

WHERE IT GROWS:

Italy: Conegliano Valdobbiadene, Asolo, Colli Euganei

Other regions: Australia, United States, New Zealand, South Africa

HOW WINE IS MADE
WHITE WINE

HARVESTING:

Grapes are picked when they're just right. Timing is key because it affects the sweetness and acidity of the grapes, which influence how the wine tastes.

CRUSHING AND PRESSING:

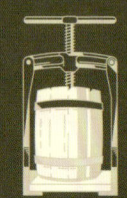

The grapes are squashed to get their juice out. The juice is separated from the grape parts for white wine right after squashing to keep the color light. White grapes have less color in their skins compared to red grapes.

FERMENTATION:

The grape juice, now called "must," is put into tanks to ferment. Stainless steel tanks are often used for white wine because they don't change the taste and keep it fresh. Yeast is added to start fermentation, turning sugar into alcohol and bubbles. Fermentation time and temperature can vary to make different styles of wine.

AGING (OPTIONAL):

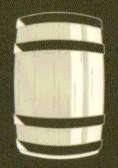

Some white wines are aged to make them taste better. This can happen in stainless steel tanks, oak barrels, or both. Oak barrels can add flavors like vanilla or spices to the wine.

BOTTLING:

Once the wine is nice and clear, it's ready to be bottled up. It gets transferred into bottles, sealed with corks or screw caps, and labeled for sale.

TOP 5 MUST - KNOW WINE REGIONS

BORDEAUX, FRANCE

Bordeaux is celebrated for its rich winemaking heritage, exceptional wines, and stunning landscapes, making it a must-visit destination for wine lovers.

GRAPE VARIETIES:

Bordeaux is famous for its red wines, which are typically blends of Cabernet Sauvignon, Merlot, Cabernet Franc, Petit Verdot, and Malbec. White Bordeaux wines are also produced, mainly from Sauvignon Blanc, Sémillon, and Muscadelle.

MOST PRESTIGIOUS WINES:

Bordeaux is home to several prestigious wine classifications, including the Bordeaux Wine Official Classification of 1855, which ranks wines from the Médoc and Sauternes. Other classifications, such as Saint-Émilion and Graves, recognize top-quality producers in those regions.

FAMOUS CHATEAUX:

Bordeaux is home to many iconic wine estates, known locally as "chateaux." These include renowned producers like Château Lafite Rothschild, Château Margaux, and Château Haut-Brion, among others.

TERROIR:

The region's diverse soils, which include gravel, limestone, and clay, contribute to the unique terroir and flavor profile of Bordeaux wines.

FOOD PAIRING:

To pair food successfully in Bordeaux, match the flavors and intensity of the wine with dishes that complement them. Whether it's a simple meal or a fancy one, Bordeaux has many delicious foods to enjoy with its top-notch wines.

RIESLING | BERRY SKIN WHITE
RHINE, GERMANY

Aromatic white wine, Riesling is popular due to its versatility and purity. It has crisp and flowery notes and a deliciously light body that accompanies a variety of foods. Sitting light on the palate, Riesling is a great option for those wanting a more aromatic white.

PRIMARY FLAVORS:

LIME | GREEN APPLE | BEESWAX | JASMINE | PEACH

AROMAS:
Jasmine, Elderflower, Lemon, Lime, Petroleum.

FINISH:
Refreshing and crisp.

PAIRS WELL WITH:
Indian Curry, Bacon, Shrimp.

TASTE PROFILE:

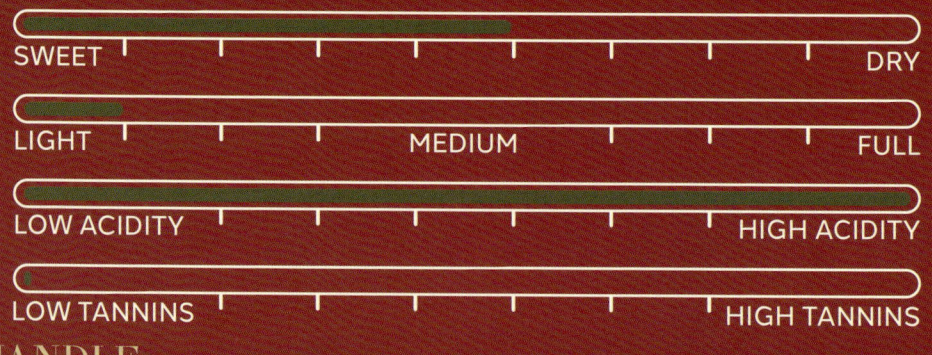

SWEET |——————————————| DRY
LIGHT |——————————————| FULL
LOW ACIDITY |——————————————| HIGH ACIDITY
LOW TANNINS |——————————————| HIGH TANNINS

HANDLE:

SERVE
38–45°F/
3–7°C

GLASS TYPE
Standard White

DECANT
No

CELLAR
3-10 years

FAMOUS FOR:
ITS INTENSE ACIDITY AND FLORAL, CITRUS AROMA.

WE RECOMMEND:
Maximin Grünhaus Maxim Riesling 2022

GRAPES:
Riesling

REGION:
Mosel Valley, Germany

WINE STYLE:
White

ALCOHOL CONTENT:
11.5%

PRICE:
£19-£24 | $20-$25

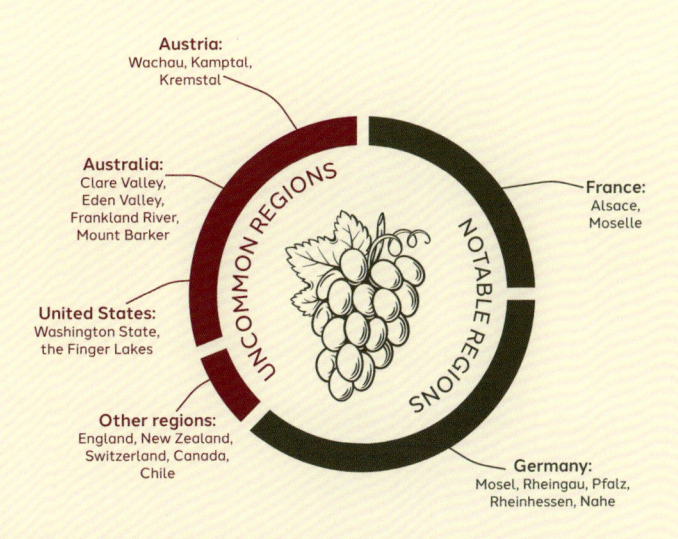

WHERE IT GROWS:

Austria:
Wachau, Kamptal, Kremstal

Australia:
Clare Valley, Eden Valley, Frankland River, Mount Barker

United States:
Washington State, the Finger Lakes

Other regions:
England, New Zealand, Switzerland, Canada, Chile

France:
Alsace, Moselle

Germany:
Mosel, Rheingau, Pfalz, Rheinhessen, Nahe

UNCOMMON REGIONS | NOTABLE REGIONS

SANGIOVESE | BERRY SKIN RED
TUSCANY, ITALY

Tuscan delicacy, Sangiovese is cherished for its savory undertones and moreish tannins, and is one of the main grapes used in Chianti. Although its specific tastes vary depending on where the grape grows, Sangiovese wine is usually earthy and juicy, with a dry and savory finish.

PRIMARY FLAVORS:

- CHERRY
- OREGANO
- ROASTED TOMATO
- BALSAMIC
- COFFEE

AROMAS:
Cherry, Raspberry, Dried Herbs, Rose, Tobacco.

FINISH:
Lingering and fruity.

PAIRS WELL WITH:
Pizza, Grilled Meats, Roasted Pepper.

TASTE PROFILE:

SWEET ——————————————●— DRY
LIGHT ————————●———— FULL
LOW ACIDITY ————————●—— HIGH ACIDITY
LOW TANNINS ——————————●—— HIGH TANNINS

HANDLE:

SERVE
60-65°F/
15-18°C

GLASS TYPE
Universal

DECANT
15-30 min

CELLAR
10-20 years

FAMOUS FOR:
ITS SHARP ACIDITY AND JUICY, HERBY NOTES.

WE RECOMMEND:
Guerrieri Galileo Colli Pesaresi Sangiovese Riserva

GRAPES:
Sangiovese

REGION:
Marche, Italy

WINE STYLE:
Red

ALCOHOL CONTENT:
14%

PRICE:
£18-£23 | $15-$20

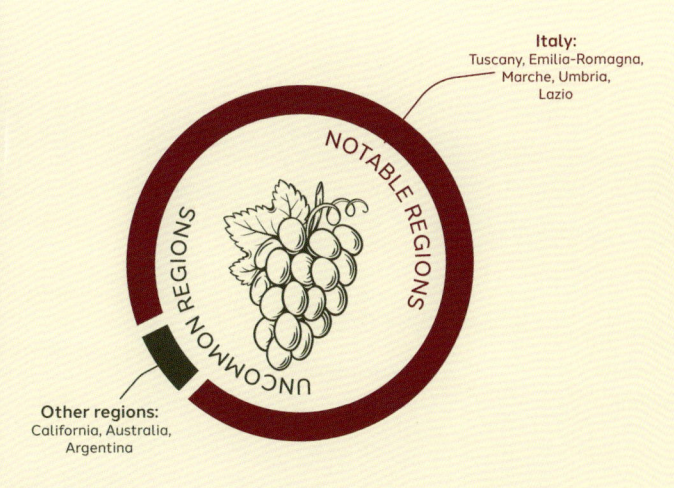

WHERE IT GROWS:

Italy:
Tuscany, Emilia-Romagna, Marche, Umbria, Lazio

Other regions:
California, Australia, Argentina

NOTABLE REGIONS
UNCOMMON REGIONS

SEKT | BERRY SKIN WHITE
RHEINGAU, GERMANY

Sekt is a German sparkling wine that is produced in a similar way to Champagne. It traditionally has a reputation for being sub-par, but a recent focus on quality has resulted in varieties of Sekt that you shouldn't ignore!

PRIMARY FLAVORS:

APPLE | PEAR | CITRUS | TOAST | JASMINE

AROMAS:
Mandarin, Apricot, Citrus, Apples, Oats.

FINISH:
Refreshing and fruity.

PAIRS WELL WITH:
Chicken, Brie, Seafood.

TASTE PROFILE:

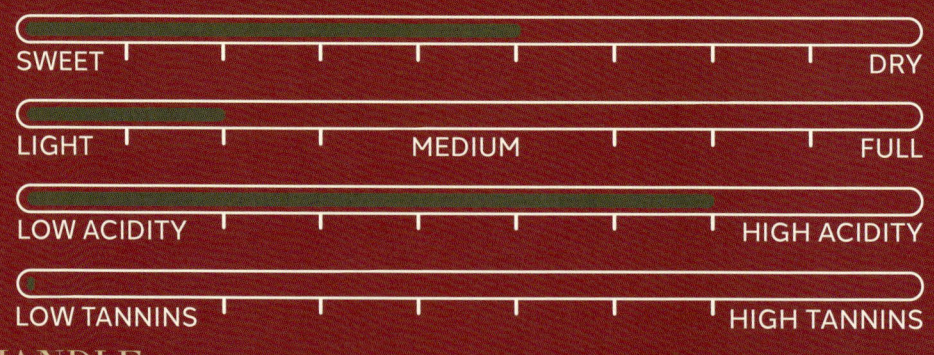

SWEET |———————————| DRY
LIGHT |———————————| FULL
LOW ACIDITY |———————————| HIGH ACIDITY
LOW TANNINS |———————————| HIGH TANNINS

HANDLE:

SERVE
45-50°F/
7-10°C

GLASS TYPE
Flute

DECANT
No

CELLAR
3-10 years

FAMOUS FOR:
ITS SWEET AND FRUITY NATURE.

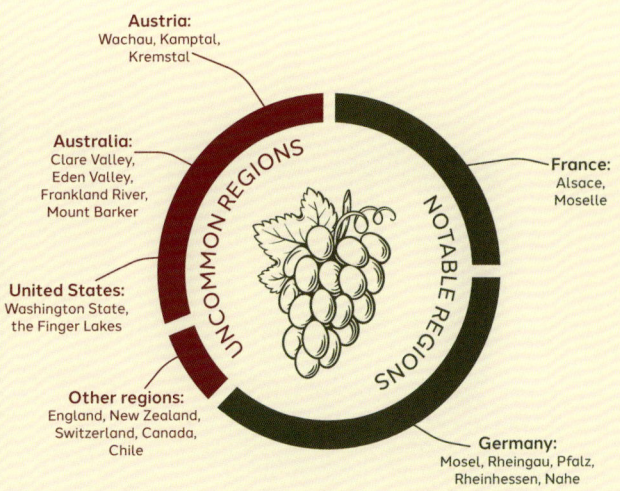

WE RECOMMEND:
Trenz Winzersekt Riesling Urgest in Brut 2018

GRAPES:
Riesling

REGION:
Rheingau, Germany

WINE STYLE:
Sparkling

ALCOHOL CONTENT:
12.5%

PRICE:
£20-£24 | $19-$24

WHERE IT GROWS:

Austria: Wachau, Kamptal, Kremstal

Australia: Clare Valley, Eden Valley, Frankland River, Mount Barker

United States: Washington State, the Finger Lakes

Other regions: England, New Zealand, Switzerland, Canada, Chile

France: Alsace, Moselle

Germany: Mosel, Rheingau, Pfalz, Rheinhessen, Nahe

UNCOMMON REGIONS / NOTABLE REGIONS

SÉMILLON | BERRY SKIN / WHITE
BORDEAUX, FRANCE

A versatile white grape, Sémillon is now grown worldwide, and is known for its range of flavors. It is commonly known for its signature floral aromatics and honeyed citrus taste, and is a great departure from your standard white wines!

PRIMARY FLAVORS:

LEMON BEESWAX CHAMOMILE PEACH HONEY

AROMAS:
Lemon, Peach, Mango, White Flower, Apricot.

FINISH:
Medium and silky.

PAIRS WELL WITH:
Shrimp, Mild Cheese, Sushi.

TASTE PROFILE:

SWEET — DRY
LIGHT — MEDIUM — FULL
LOW ACIDITY — HIGH ACIDITY
LOW TANNINS — HIGH TANNINS

HANDLE:

SERVE
45-55°F/
7-12°C

GLASS TYPE
Standard White

DECANT
15 Mins

CELLAR
5-10 years

FAMOUS FOR:
ITS COMPLEX DEPTH AND RICH SILKINESS.

WE RECOMMEND:
Vergelegen Semillon Straw 2021

GRAPES:
Sémillon

REGION:
Stellenbosch, South Africa

WINE STYLE:
White

ALCOHOL CONTENT:
12%

PRICE:
£16-£19 | $18-$21

WHERE IT GROWS:

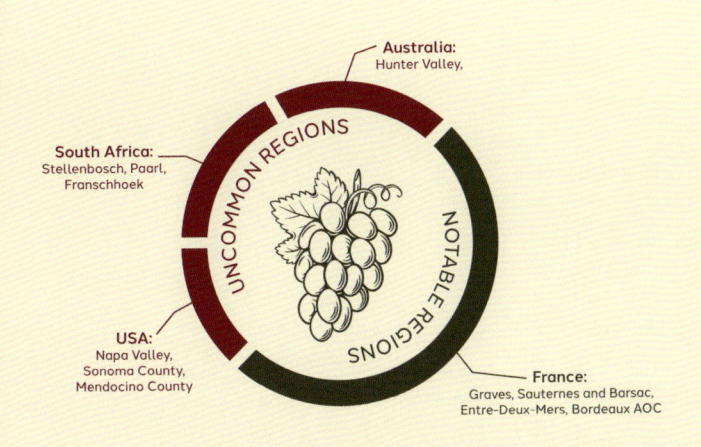

Australia: Hunter Valley,

South Africa: Stellenbosch, Paarl, Franschhoek

USA: Napa Valley, Sonoma County, Mendocino County

France: Graves, Sauternes and Barsac, Entre-Deux-Mers, Bordeaux AOC

UNCOMMON REGIONS | NOTABLE REGIONS

HOW WINE IS MADE
RED WINE

HARVESTING:

Grapes are picked when they're fully ripe. This affects the sugar and acid levels in the grapes, which influence the wine's flavor.

CRUSHING AND PRESSING:

Grapes are crushed to release their juice and skins. Some remove the stems to avoid bitterness.

FERMENTATION:

Yeast is added to the must (juice with skins) to initiate fermentation. During fermentation, sugars in the juice are converted into alcohol and carbon dioxide. Fermentation temperatures and duration can vary depending on the desired style of wine.

AGING:

Red wine is often aged in oak barrels to develop additional complexity, flavors, and aromas. Oak barrels can impart characteristics such as vanilla, spice, and toastiness to the wine. Aging times can vary depending on the style of wine and the winemaker's preferences.

BOTTLING:

Once the wine has aged to perfection, it is bottled, sealed with corks or screw caps, and labeled for sale. Red wines may continue to develop in the bottle over time, so they can be enjoyed immediately or cellared for aging.

OF COURSE SIZE MATTERS, NO ONE WANTS A SMALL GLASS OF WINE

SOAVE | BERRY SKIN WHITE
VENETO, ITALY

Known for its toasty, almond-tinged acidity, Soave is primarily made from Garganega grapes. Dry and lean, this delicious white wine is perfectly balanced in-between fruitiness, salinity, tartness, and richness.

PRIMARY FLAVORS:

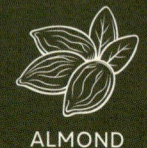

- PEACH
- HONEYDEW MELON
- TANGERINE
- ALMOND
- GREEN APPLE

AROMAS:
White Flowers, Lemon, Marjoram, Almond, Tangerine.

FINISH:
Crisp and mineral.

PAIRS WELL WITH:
Bruschetta, White Fish, Chicken.

TASTE PROFILE:

SWEET —————————————————— DRY
LIGHT —————————————————— FULL (MEDIUM)
LOW ACIDITY —————————————————— HIGH ACIDITY
LOW TANNINS —————————————————— HIGH TANNINS

HANDLE:

SERVE
45–55°F/
7–12°C

GLASS TYPE
Standard White

DECANT
No

CELLAR
3–7 years

FAMOUS FOR:
ITS MELON AND CITRUS FLAVOR, AND MINERAL FINISH.

WE RECOMMEND:
Monte Tondo Mito Soave 2022

GRAPES:
Garganega

REGION:
Veneto, Italy

WINE STYLE:
White

ALCOHOL CONTENT:
12%

PRICE:
£14-£16 | $13-$17

WHERE IT GROWS:

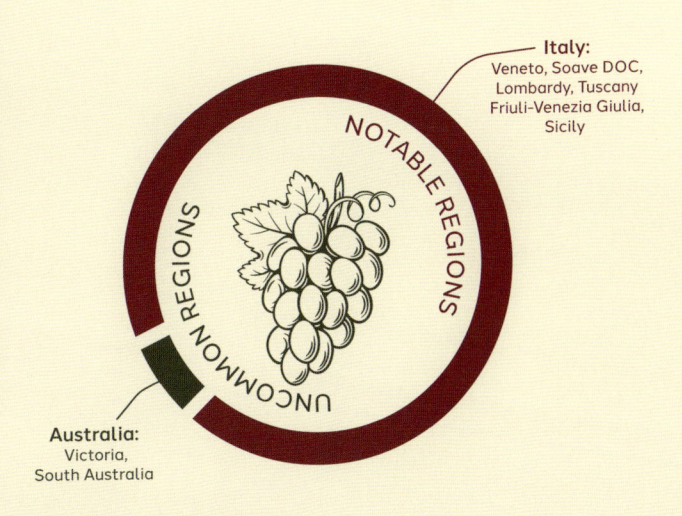

Italy: Veneto, Soave DOC, Lombardy, Tuscany, Friuli-Venezia Giulia, Sicily

Australia: Victoria, South Australia

(NOTABLE REGIONS / UNCOMMON REGIONS)

TOKAJI ASZÚ | BERRY SKIN WHITE
TOKAJ-HEGYALJA, HUNGARY

Hungary's most famous sweet wine, renowned for its unique taste profile. This is made from grapes that are affected by a particular type of root rot that alters the taste and concentrates the sugars, creating a very unique and delicious sweet wine!

PRIMARY FLAVORS:
- HONEY 
- ORANGE 
- APRICOT 
- GINGER 
- MARZIPAN 

AROMAS:
Lemon, Mint, Honey, Pepper, Tobacco, Nougat.

FINISH:
Long and sweet.

PAIRS WELL WITH:
Blue Cheese, Caramel, Hazelnut.

TASTE PROFILE:
- SWEET —— DRY
- LIGHT —— MEDIUM —— FULL
- LOW ACIDITY —— HIGH ACIDITY
- LOW TANNINS —— HIGH TANNINS

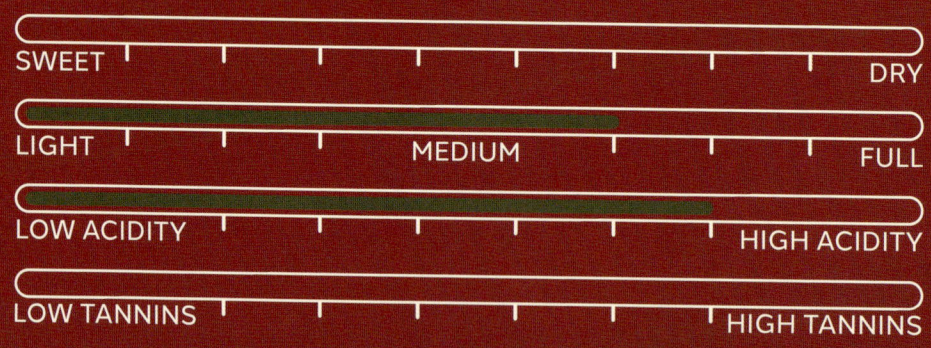

HANDLE:
- **SERVE**: 45–55°F / 7–12°C
- **GLASS TYPE**: Sweet Wine 
- **DECANT**: No 
- **CELLAR**: 10-20 years

FAMOUS FOR:
ITS DECADENT SWEETNESS AND RICH NOTES.

WE RECOMMEND:
Tokaji PDO Aszú 5 Puttonyos 2016
Samuel Tinon

GRAPES:
Furmint 90%, Hárslevelű 10%

REGION:
Tokaj-Hegyalja, Hungary

WINE STYLE:
Sweet

ALCOHOL CONTENT:
11.5%

PRICE:
£27-£35 | $37-$45

WHERE IT GROWS:

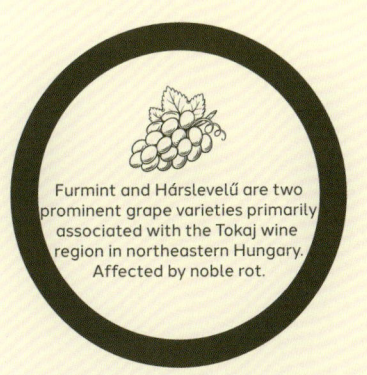

Furmint and Hárslevelű are two prominent grape varieties primarily associated with the Tokaj wine region in northeastern Hungary. Affected by noble rot.

Furmint and Hárslevelű are closely associated with the Tokaj wine region in Hungary, where they are cultivated in vineyards situated on volcanic slopes overlooking the Bodrog and Tisza rivers. Together, they contribute to the unique character and reputation of Tokaji wines, showcasing the rich winemaking heritage of the region.

TORRONTÉS | BERRY SKIN WHITE
SALTA, ARGENTINA

A delicious Argentinian white that is known for its intense aromatic profile and medium-light body. Perfect for fans of Moscato or Riesling, Torrontés is a great alternative for those wanting a fruity and floral white that is perfect all year round!

PRIMARY FLAVORS:

PEACH | LEMON | PINEAPPLE | ROSE | ORANGE BLOSSO

AROMAS:
Orange Blossom, Rose, Jasmine, Pear, Lychee.

FINISH:
Crisp and floral.

PAIRS WELL WITH:
Seafood, Creamy Pasta, Curry.

TASTE PROFILE:

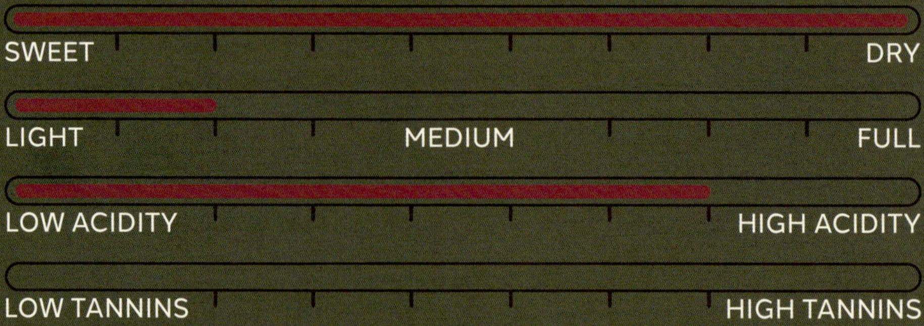

SWEET —————————————————— DRY
LIGHT —————————————————— FULL
LOW ACIDITY —————————————————— HIGH ACIDITY
LOW TANNINS —————————————————— HIGH TANNINS

HANDLE:

SERVE
38–45°F/
3–7°C

GLASS TYPE
Standard White

DECANT
No

CELLAR
1–3 years

FAMOUS FOR:
ITS FRUITY, SEMI-SWEET AND BALANCED NATURE

WE RECOMMEND:
Valles Calchaquìes IG Torrontés 2022 El Esteco

GRAPES:
Torrontés

REGION:
Salta, Argentina

WINE STYLE:
White

ALCOHOL CONTENT:
13.5%

PRICE:
£14-£17 | $13-$16

WHERE IT GROWS:

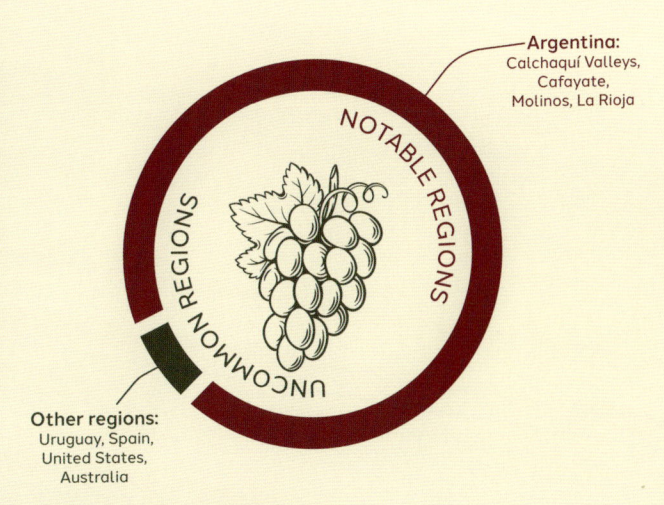

Argentina: Calchaquí Valleys, Cafayate, Molinos, La Rioja

Other regions: Uruguay, Spain, United States, Australia

NOTABLE REGIONS / UNCOMMON REGIONS

TVISHI | BERRY SKIN WHITE
SAMEGRELO, GEORGIA

A unique Georgian white wine made from the Tsolikouri grape that is characterised by its medium body and distinct aromas. Light straw in color, this wine may be slightly rarer, but perfect if you want a white wine with a little more body and balanced sweetness!

PRIMARY FLAVORS:

GREEN APPLE — **PEAR** — **HONEY** — **QUINCE** — **WHITE FLOWER**

AROMAS:
Honeysuckle, Apricot, Quince, Pineapple, Mint.

FINISH:
Crisp and fruity.

PAIRS WELL WITH:
Light Cheese, Fish, Grilled Meat.

TASTE PROFILE:

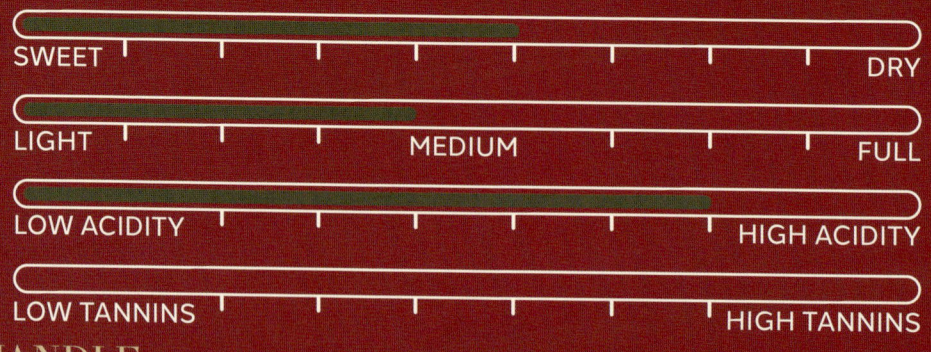

SWEET ——————————————— DRY
LIGHT ———— MEDIUM ———— FULL
LOW ACIDITY ——————————— HIGH ACIDITY
LOW TANNINS ——————————— HIGH TANNINS

HANDLE:

SERVE
45-50°F/
7-10°C

GLASS TYPE
Standard White

DECANT
No

CELLAR
No

FAMOUS FOR:
ITS FRUITY, SEMI-SWEET AND BALANCED NATURE.

WE RECOMMEND:
Marani Tvishi 2021

GRAPES:
Tsolikauri

REGION:
Racha-Lechkhumi, Georgia

WINE STYLE:
White

ALCOHOL CONTENT:
11%

PRICE:
£14-£17 | $27-$33

WHERE IT GROWS:

Tsolikauri is a white grape variety native to the country of Georgia, specifically to the western part of the country, particularly in the region of Imereti.

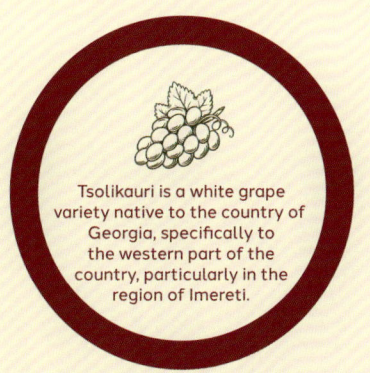

Tsolikauri is one of the indigenous Georgian grape varieties that contribute to the country's vibrant wine culture and the production of traditional Georgian wines. It is often used to produce crisp and aromatic white wines, either as a varietal wine or as part of blends.

OH LOOK
—IT'S—
Wine
O'CLOCK

TOP 10 MUST KNOW WINE REGIONS

NAPA VALLEY, USA

Napa Valley's scenic beauty, world-class wines, and vibrant culinary culture make it a premier destination for wine enthusiasts and travelers alike.

GRAPE VARIETIES:
Napa Valley is known for producing high-quality wines, particularly from Bordeaux grape varieties such as Cabernet Sauvignon, Merlot, and Cabernet Franc for red wines, and Chardonnay and Sauvignon Blanc for white wines.

WINE STYLES:
Napa Valley produces a wide range of wine styles, from bold and opulent Cabernet Sauvignon to crisp and refreshing Sauvignon Blanc. The region is also known for its innovative winemaking techniques, such as barrel aging and blending, which add complexity and depth to the wines.

KEY WINE REGIONS:
Napa Valley is divided into several subregions, each with its own microclimate: Stags Leap District, Oakville, Rutherford, Yountville.

TERROIR:
Napa Valley's terroir combines a favorable climate, diverse soils, varied topography, ample sunlight, and reliable water sources to create optimal growing conditions for producing high-quality wines.

FOOD PAIRING:
Napa Valley wines pair well with a variety of dishes, including grilled meats, roasted vegetables, artisan cheeses, and decadent desserts. The region's diverse culinary scene offers plenty of opportunities to enjoy wine and food pairings at acclaimed restaurants and wineries.

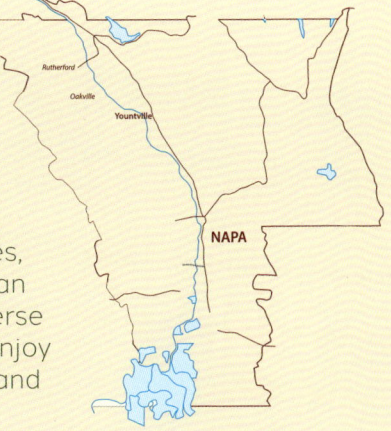

HOW WINE IS MADE
ROSÉ WINE

HARVESTING:

Grapes are picked when they're ripe, similar to those for red or white wine production.

CRUSHING AND PRESSING:

Grapes are crushed to release their juice. The skins remain in contact with the juice for a shorter period compared to red wine production. After maceration, the juice is pressed off the skins. The longer the skins are in contact with the juice, the deeper the color of the resulting rosé.

FERMENTATION:

The juice, now separated from the skins, undergoes fermentation. Fermentation can occur in stainless steel tanks, barrels, or other vessels.

AGING (OPTIONAL):

Some rosé wines may undergo a short period of aging, typically in stainless steel tanks, to preserve the freshness and fruitiness of the wine.

BOTTLING:

Once fermentation and any optional aging or blending processes are complete, the rosé wine is bottled, sealed, and labeled for sale.

Given ENOUGH *Wine* I COULD *Rule* THE WORLD

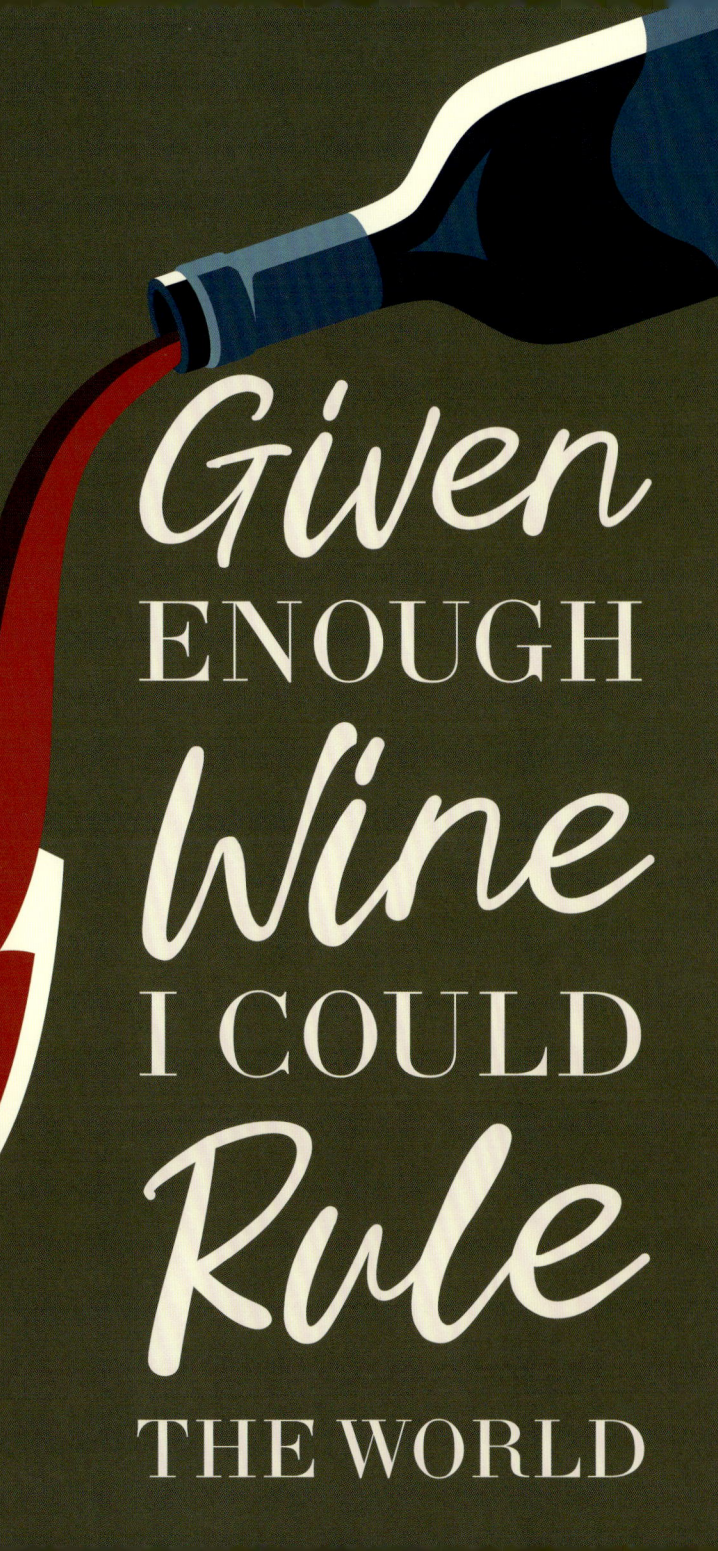

VERDEJO | BERRY SKIN WHITE

RUEDA, SPAIN

Citrus and herbs dominate this Spanish white wine, grown almost exclusively in the Rueda region of Spain. A great alternative to Pinot Grigio and Sauvignon Blanc, but with the ability to age with a rich and deep flavor, which is balanced out by its zippy bitterness.

PRIMARY FLAVORS:

LIME HONEYDEW MELON FENNEL PINEAPPLE GRAPEFRUIT

AROMAS:
Citrus, Grass, Fennel, Jasmine, Honeysuckle.

FINISH:
Mineral and crisp.

PAIRS WELL WITH:
Fish, Chimichurri, Grilled Chicken.

TASTE PROFILE:

SWEET ——————————————— DRY

LIGHT —— MEDIUM —— FULL

LOW ACIDITY ——————————————— HIGH ACIDITY

LOW TANNINS ——————————————— HIGH TANNINS

HANDLE:

SERVE
38–45°F/
3–7°C

GLASS TYPE
Standard White

DECANT
No

CELLAR
1–3 years

FAMOUS FOR:
ITS AROMATIC PROFILE AND CRISP ACIDITY.

WE RECOMMEND:
Javier Sanz Viticultor Verdejo 2022

GRAPES:
Verdejo

REGION:
Rueda, Spain

WINE STYLE:
White

ALCOHOL CONTENT:
13%

PRICE:
£15-£17 | $12-$16

WHERE IT GROWS:

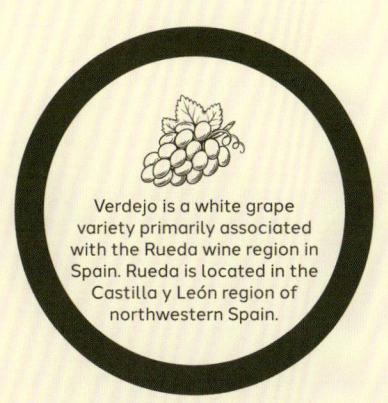

Verdejo is a white grape variety primarily associated with the Rueda wine region in Spain. Rueda is located in the Castilla y León region of northwestern Spain.

While Rueda is the primary region associated with Verdejo cultivation, the grape variety is also grown in smaller quantities in other regions of Spain, such as Tierra de León and Toro. However, Rueda remains the most renowned and significant region for Verdejo production.

VINHO VERDE | BERRY SKIN WHITE
MINHO PROVINCE, PORTUGAL

Vinho Verde, a renowned white wine from Portugal, is celebrated for its light and refreshing character. This wine delights the palate with its subtle effervescence, sharp acidity and brightness. Made primarily from the Loureiro grape, a great option for a unique and delicious drinking experience!

PRIMARY FLAVORS:

LEMON · LIME · GRAPEFRUIT · GOOSEBERRY · WHITE BLOSSOM

AROMAS:
Lemon, Lime, Green Apple, White Blossom, Grassy.

FINISH:
Crisp and acidic.

PAIRS WELL WITH:
Sushi, Citrus Salads, Chicken.

TASTE PROFILE:

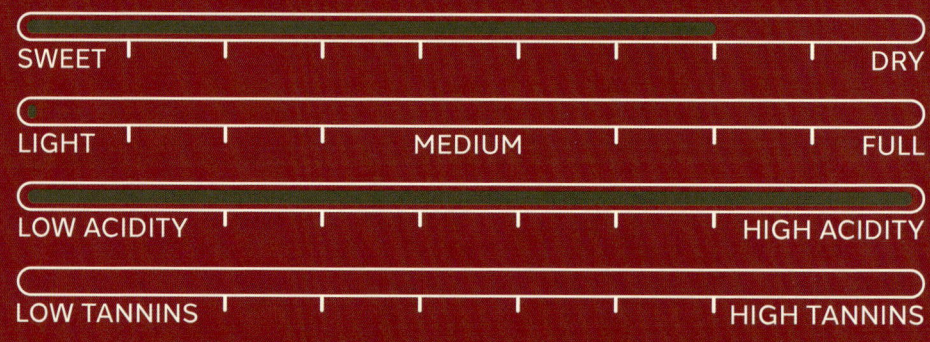

SWEET ———————————————●— DRY
LIGHT —●——————————————— FULL
LOW ACIDITY ————————————————●— HIGH ACIDITY
LOW TANNINS ——————————————————— HIGH TANNINS

HANDLE:

SERVE
38–45°F/
3–7°C

GLASS TYPE
Standard White

DECANT
No

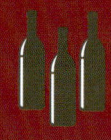

CELLAR
1-2 years

FAMOUS FOR:
ITS MOUTH-WATERING ACIDITY AND SUBTLE CARBONATION.

WE RECOMMEND:
Vila Nova Vinho Verde 2022

GRAPES:
Loureiro, Arinto

REGION:
Penafiel, Portugal

WINE STYLE:
White

ALCOHOL CONTENT:
11%

PRICE:
£9-£12 | $10-$13

WHERE IT GROWS:

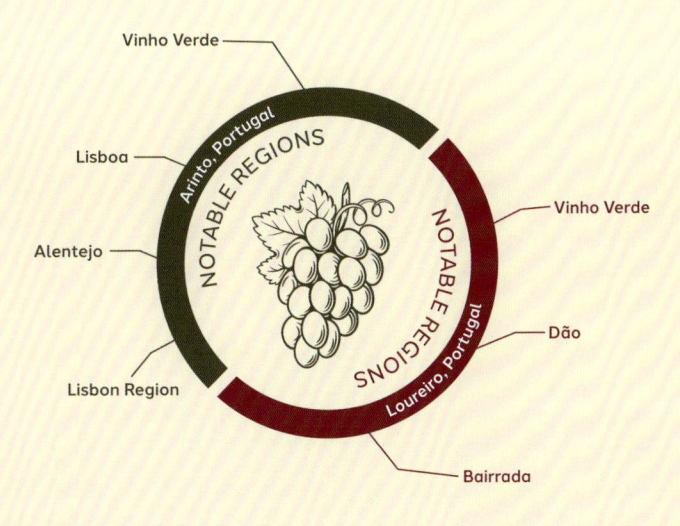

- Vinho Verde
- Lisboa
- Alentejo
- Lisbon Region

NOTABLE REGIONS — Arinto, Portugal

NOTABLE REGIONS — Loureiro, Portugal
- Vinho Verde
- Dão
- Bairrada

- 89 -

VINSANTO | BERRY SKIN WHITE
SANTORINI, GREECE

Hailing from the sunny Greek island of Santorini, this sweet wine is made from sun-dried grapes. It has an earthy, dried fruit taste and subtle yet complex spices and caramelization to make it a delicious and unique dessert wine!

PRIMARY FLAVORS:

RAISIN — ROASTED PEPPER — HONEY — CARAMEL — CINNAMON

AROMAS:
Bergamot, Honey, Cinnamon, Clove, Raisin.

FINISH:
Sweet and velvety.

PAIRS WELL WITH:
Baklava, Dried Fruits, Almonds.

TASTE PROFILE:

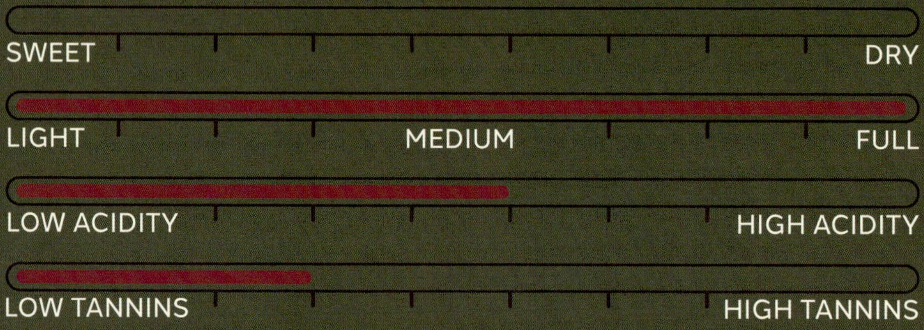

SWEET — DRY
LIGHT — MEDIUM — FULL
LOW ACIDITY — HIGH ACIDITY
LOW TANNINS — HIGH TANNINS

HANDLE:

- **SERVE**: 55–60°F / 12–15°C
- **GLASS TYPE**: Sweet Wine
- **DECANT**: No 
- **CELLAR**: 10+ years

FAMOUS FOR:
ITS LUSCIOUS SWEETNESS, VIBRANT ACIDITY AND A RANGE OF FLAVORS.

WE RECOMMEND:
Santo Wines Santorini Vinsanto 2017

GRAPES:
Assyrtiko 85% & Aidani 15%

REGION:
Santorini, Greece

WINE STYLE:
Sweet

ALCOHOL CONTENT:
13%

PRICE:
£30-£35 | $38-$43

WHERE IT GROWS:

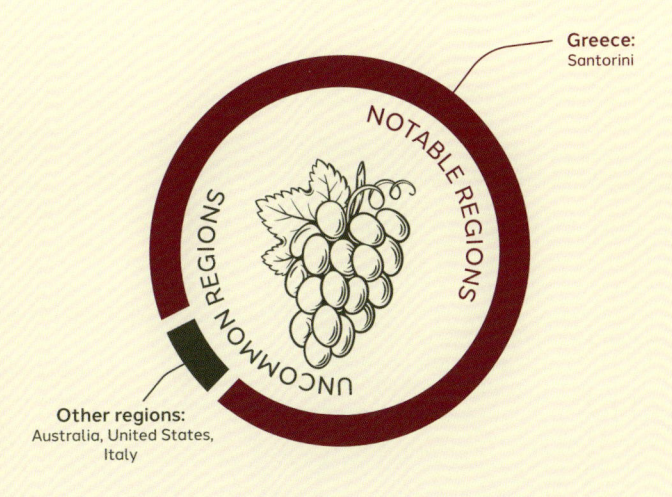

Greece: Santorini

Other regions: Australia, United States, Italy

ZWEIGELT | BERRY SKIN RED
KLOSTERNEUBURG, AUSTRIA

Primarily grown in Austria, Zweigelt is a medium bodied wine that is filled with juicy, fruit-forward flavor. Similar to Pinot Noir, this wine is beautifully bright and tart, resulting in a lighter red wine that doesn't fall short on taste!

PRIMARY FLAVORS:
- CHERRY 
- RASPBERRY 
- CRANBERRY 
- BLACK PEPPER 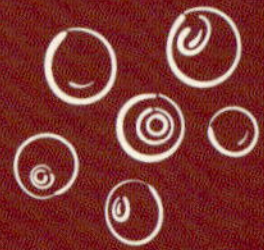
- VIOLET 

AROMAS:
Cherry, Raspberry, Cinnamon, Dill, Black Pepper.

FINISH:
Medium and fruity.

PAIRS WELL WITH:
Roast Chicken, Camembert, Light Pasta.

TASTE PROFILE:
- Sweet ——————————————●—— Dry
- Light ————●———————— Full
- Low Acidity ——————————●—— High Acidity
- Low Tannins ————●———————— High Tannins

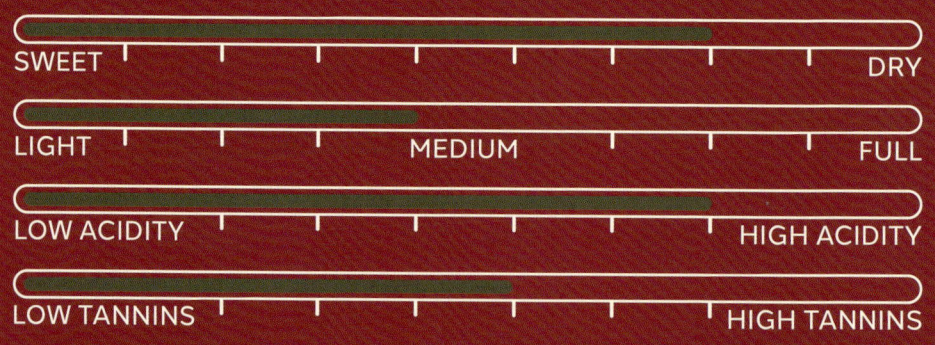

HANDLE:
- **SERVE**: 55-60°F / 12-15°C
- **GLASS TYPE**: Burgundy 
- **DECANT**: 30 mins 
- **CELLAR**: 3-5 years

FAMOUS FOR:
SOUR FRUIT TASTE AND SMOOTH FINISH.

WE RECOMMEND:
Weingut R&A Pfaffl Austrian Cherry Zweigelt 2022

GRAPES:
Zweigelt

REGION
Niederosterreich, Austria

WINE STYLE:
Red

ALCOHOL CONTENT:
13.5%

PRICE:
£12-£15 | $14-$17

WHERE IT GROWS:

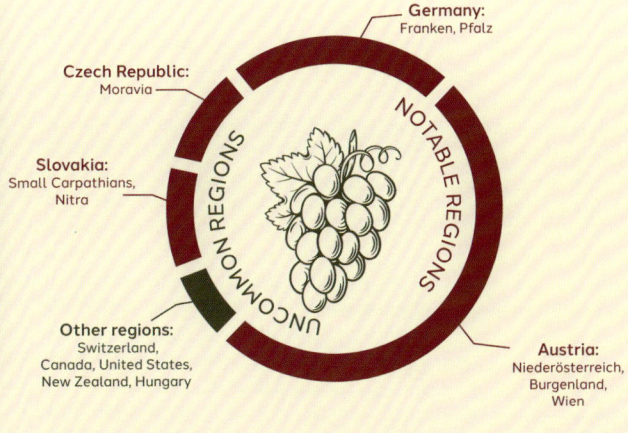

Germany: Franken, Pfalz

Czech Republic: Moravia

Slovakia: Small Carpathians, Nitra

Other regions: Switzerland, Canada, United States, New Zealand, Hungary

Austria: Niederösterreich, Burgenland, Wien

NOTABLE REGIONS / UNCOMMON REGIONS

VINO VOCAB

These are just a few examples of wine vocabulary terms used. They're a small taste of the colorful language swirling around the vineyard, describing all hidden gems in every glass.

ACIDITY:
Letting wine sit in barrels, tanks, or bottles to get more flavorful over time.

APPELLATION:
A fancy term for the special place where grapes grow and wine is made, usually with strict rules about quality.

BODY:
How heavy or light wine feels in your mouth, from light to heavy.

BOUQUET:
The fancy smell of an older wine, made more complex by sitting in bottles for a while.

CORKED:
When wine tastes unpleasant because the cork caused it to spoil.

DECANTING:
Pouring wine into a fancy glass pitcher to remove any undesirable elements and allow it to aerate.

FERMENTATION:
How grape juice turns into wine, thanks to tiny yeast creatures.

FINISH:
The lingering flavor that remains after you've finished your glass of wine.

OAK:
Adding flavor to wine by aging it in oak barrels, like a spicy, toasty, vanilla touch.

TANNINS:
The stuff in wine that makes your mouth feel dry, found in grape skins, seeds, and stems.

TERROIR:
Fancy word for how the land and weather where grapes grow affect the taste of wine.

VARIETAL:
Wine made mostly from one type of grape, like Cabernet Sauvignon or Chardonnay.

VINTAGE:
The year grapes were picked, telling you how good the wine might be.

LEGS:
Those lines on the side of the glass after you swirl wine around, showing how thick or boozy it is.

MOUTHFEEL:
How wine feels in your mouth, like smooth, rough, or thick.

NOSE:
The fancy smell of wine, checked by taking a big sniff before drinking.

SPARKLING:
Wine with bubbles, like Champagne or Prosecco, to make things fun and fizzy.

CABERNET SAUVIGNON
FRANCE | WINE TYPE: RED

Originating in Bordeaux, Cabernet Sauvignon is now one of the most widely planted grape varieties worldwide due to its adaptability. Traditionally grown in Bordeaux, France, it is also extensively cultivated in New World regions like California and Chile.

PRIMARY FLAVORS:

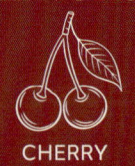

BLACK FRUIT | **CHERRY** | **PLUM** | **CEDAR** | **MINT**

AROMAS:
Dark Spices, Cedarwood, Blackcurrant, Black Pepper.

FINISH:
Rich dark fruit flavors, savory undertones and balanced acidity.

PAIRS WELL WITH:
Red Meat, Nutty Cheese, Portobello Mushrooms.

TASTE PROFILE:

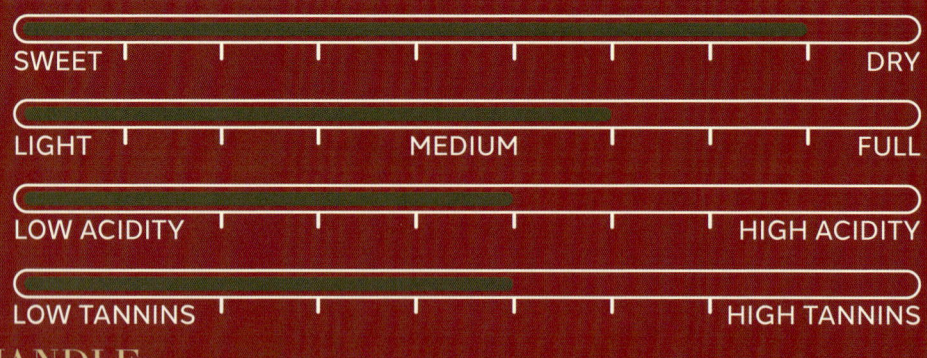

SWEET |—————————————————————| DRY

LIGHT |—————— MEDIUM ——————| FULL

LOW ACIDITY |—————————————| HIGH ACIDITY

LOW TANNINS |—————————————| HIGH TANNINS

HANDLE:

SERVE	GLASS TYPE	DECANT	CELLAR
55°-65°F/ 15°-18°C	Standard Red	2-3 hours	5-15 years

FAMOUS FOR:

ITS EXCEPTIONAL DEPTH AND COMPLEX FLAVORS.

OUR TOP 15 WINES TO TRY!

WE RECOMMEND:
Xavier Roger Big Beltie Cabernet Sauvignon 2022

GRAPES:
Cabernet Sauvignon

REGION:
Languedoc-Roussillon, France

WINE STYLE:
French Cabernet Sauvignon

ALCOHOL CONTENT:
13.5%

PRICE:
£10-£11 | $14-$15

BRUT CHAMPAGNE
FRANCE | WINE TYPE: SPARKLING

Champagne is the name given to certain sparkling wines that are made in the Champagne region of France. Champagne may be made from a range of grape varieties, including Chardonnay, Pinot Meunier and Pinot Noir!

PRIMARY FLAVORS:

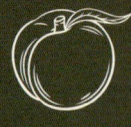

PEACH — **CREAM** — **CITRUS** — **ALMOND** — **TOAST**

AROMAS:
Apple, Citrus, White Flower, Baked Bread, Chalk.

FINISH:
Vibrant acidity, fine bubbles and refreshing fruit flavors.

PAIRS WELL WITH:
Mushrooms, Seafood, Popcorn.

TASTE PROFILE:

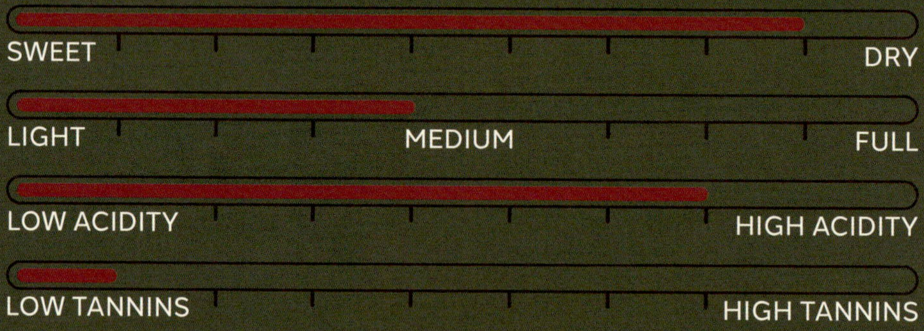

SWEET ———————————————————————— DRY

LIGHT ——————— MEDIUM ——————— FULL

LOW ACIDITY ———————————————— HIGH ACIDITY

LOW TANNINS ———————————————— HIGH TANNINS

HANDLE:

SERVE
48°-54°F/
9°-12°C

GLASS TYPE
Tulip

DECANT
No

CELLAR
No

FAMOUS FOR:

ITS CREAMY, CRISP FINISH, AND BEING THE MOST FAMOUS WINE IN THE WORLD!

OUR TOP 15 WINES TO TRY!

WE RECOMMEND:
Duménil Grande Réserve Brut Champagne Premier Cru

GRAPES:
Chardonnay, Pinot Noir, Pinot Meunier

REGION:
Champagne, France

WINE STYLE:
Sparkling

ALCOHOL CONTENT:
12%

PRICE:
£30-£40 | $35-$45

CHARDONNAY
CALIFORNIA | WINE TYPE: WHITE

Originating in Burgundy, Chardonnay has since become world renowned, and its New World home in California, USA, has great options on a budget! It has an extremely varied taste, ranging from dry and citrusy to toasty and exotic.

PRIMARY FLAVORS:

VANILLA | PINEAPPLE | GUAVA | PAPAYA | MANGO

AROMAS:
Green Apple, Lemon Zest, Butter, Mango, Nuttiness.

FINISH:
Creamy texture, ripe fruit flavors and subtle oak.

PAIRS WELL WITH:
Lobster, Chicken, Nuts.

TASTE PROFILE:

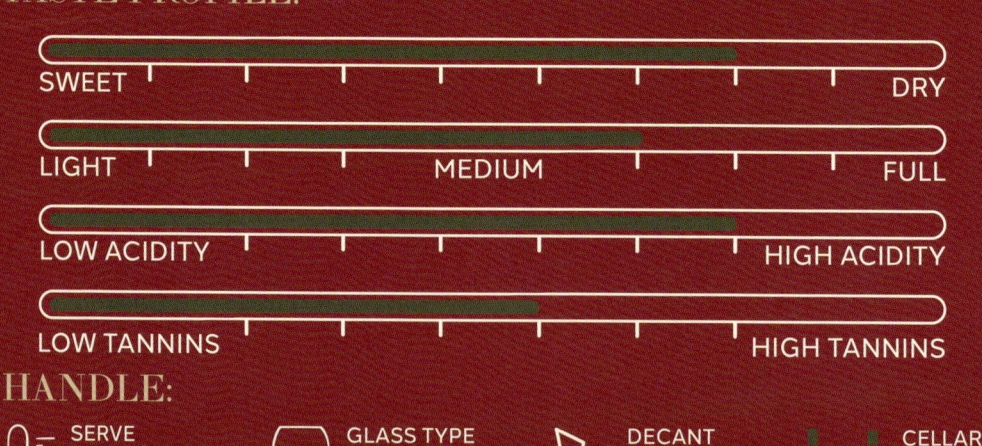

SWEET —————————————————— DRY

LIGHT ———— MEDIUM ———— FULL

LOW ACIDITY —————————————— HIGH ACIDITY

LOW TANNINS —————————————— HIGH TANNINS

HANDLE:

SERVE
55-60 °F/
13-16 °C

GLASS TYPE
Burgundy

DECANT
30 mins

CELLAR
No

FAMOUS FOR:

ITS VERSATILITY, WITH A VAST FLAVOR PROFILE RANGING FROM CRISP TO RICH AND BUTTERY.

OUR TOP 15 WINES TO TRY!

WE RECOMMEND:
Avalon Chardonnay 2021

GRAPES:
Chardonnay

REGION:
Graton, California

WINE STYLE:
White

ALCOHOL CONTENT:
13.5%

PRICE:
£13-£16 | $10-$15

CHENIN BLANC
SOUTH AFRICA | WINE TYPE: WHITE

The New World Chenin Blanc, produced in South Africa as opposed to its traditional home in France's Loire Valley, has rich, concentrated flavors of tropical fruits and honey.

PRIMARY FLAVORS:

| APPLE | PEAR | PEACH | PINEAPPLE | LEMON |

AROMAS:
Pear-drop, Peach, Honey, Floral.

FINISH:
Refreshing acidity and vibrant fruit flavors.

PAIRS WELL WITH:
Vegetables, Goat's Cheese, Charcuterie.

TASTE PROFILE:

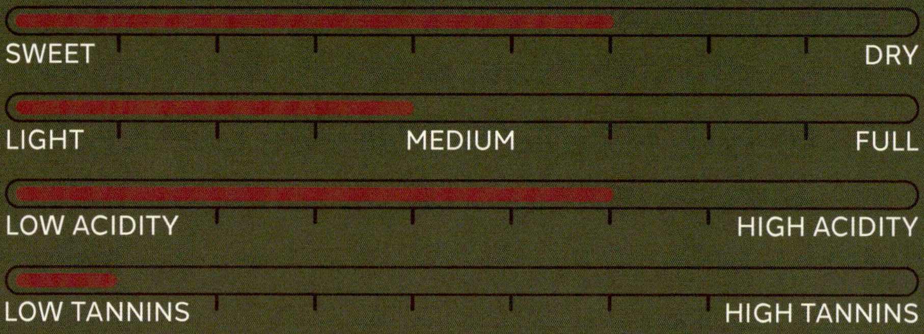

SWEET ———————————————— DRY

LIGHT ——— MEDIUM ——— FULL

LOW ACIDITY ———————————————— HIGH ACIDITY

LOW TANNINS ———————————————— HIGH TANNINS

HANDLE:

SERVE	GLASS TYPE	DECANT	CELLAR
44-50°F/ 7-10 °C	Standard White	5-15 mins	3-5 years

FAMOUS FOR:

ITS FRUIT NOTES AND A CLEAN FINISH, WITH DEPTH AND BODY.

OUR TOP 15 WINES TO TRY!

WE RECOMMEND:
Brookdale Estate Mason Road Chenin Blanc 2021

GRAPES:
Chenin Blanc

REGION:
Paarl, South Africa

WINE STYLE
South African Chenin Blanc

ALCOHOL CONTENT:
13.5%

PRICE:
£14-£18 | $10-$15

CRÉMANT DE LIMOUX
FRANCE | WINE TYPE: SPARKLING

Crémant is a style of French sparkling wine that is made in the same way as Champagne, but produced in other regions. Crémant and Champagne are fermented in the bottles rather than in tanks, as is the case with other sparkling wines!

PRIMARY FLAVORS:

HONEY | APPLE BLOSSOM | PASTRY | ALMONDS | LIME

AROMAS:
White Flower, Green Apple, Citrus, Yeast.

FINISH:
Crisp acidity, bright fruit flavors.

PAIRS WELL WITH:
White Fish, Salted Fries, Charcuterie.

TASTE PROFILE:

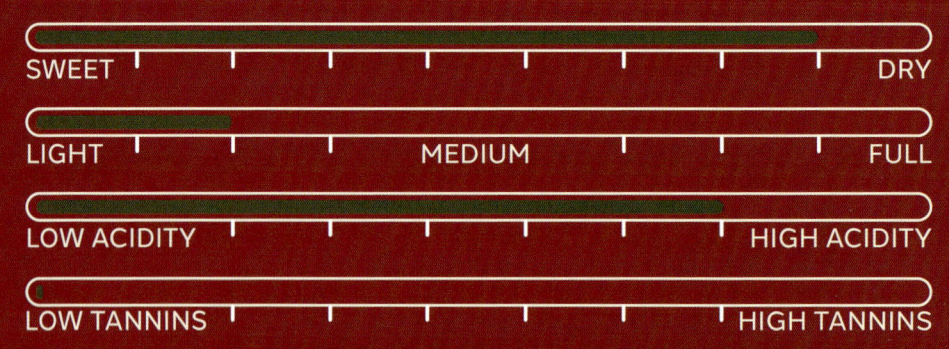

SWEET |——————————————————————| DRY

LIGHT |——————————————————————| FULL

LOW ACIDITY |——————————————————————| HIGH ACIDITY

LOW TANNINS |——————————————————————| HIGH TANNINS

HANDLE:

SERVE
48°-54°F/
9°-12°C

GLASS TYPE
Tulip

DECANT
No

CELLAR
No

FAMOUS FOR:

CHAMPAGNE'S TOASTY NOTES, WITHOUT THE CHAMPAGNE PRICE TAG.

OUR TOP 15 WINES TO TRY!

WE RECOMMEND:
Antech Cremant de Limoux
Cuvee Eugenie Brut

GRAPES:
Chardonnay, Chenin Blanc, Mauzac

REGION:
Languedoc-Roussillon, France

WINE STYLE:
Crémant

ALCOHOL CONTENT:
12%

PRICE:
£13-£18 | $18-$25

HOW WINE IS MADE
SPARKLING WINE

BASE WINE PRODUCTION:
Grapes are harvested and turned into a base wine through the usual process of crushing, fermentation, and aging. The base wine is usually dry and low in alcohol.

BLENDING:
In some cases, different batches of base wine may be blended together to achieve the desired flavor profile and consistency.

SECONDARY FERMENTATION:
The base wine is transferred to a pressurized tank or bottle, along with a mixture of yeast and sugar (known as the liqueur de tirage). The yeast consumes the added sugar, producing alcohol and carbon dioxide as byproducts. This secondary fermentation happens in the sealed container, trapping the carbon dioxide in the wine, creating bubbles.

AGING:
The wine undergoes aging on its lees (dead yeast cells) to develop complexity and flavor. The length of aging can vary, but it typically lasts for several months to several years.

BOTTLING:
The bottles are corked, and aged further, allowing the flavors to meld and mature. Finally, the bottles are sealed, labeled, and ready for sale.

TOP 5 MUST KNOW WINE REGIONS

STELLENBOSCH, CAPE TOWN

Stellenbosch is celebrated for its picturesque vineyard landscapes, rich viticultural heritage, and exceptional wines that reflect the region's unique terroir and winemaking traditions.

GRAPE VARIETIES:

Stellenbosch is known for producing a wide range of grape varieties, including Cabernet Sauvignon, Merlot, Shiraz, and Chardonnay. However, it's particularly renowned for its premium red wines made from Bordeaux varietals like Cabernet Sauvignon and Merlot.

WINE STYLES:

Stellenbosch produces a diverse array of wine styles, from rich and full-bodied reds to crisp and aromatic whites. The region is particularly famous for its bold and expressive Cabernet Sauvignon wines, which showcase the terroir and craftsmanship of Stellenbosch winemakers.

KEY WINE REGIONS:

Stellenbosch, South Africa, is one of the country's premier wine regions and is divided into several subregions, each with its own microclimate, Stellenbosch Valley, Helderberg, Banghoek Valley, Jonkershoek Valley, Simonsberg-Stellenbosch.

TERROIR:

Stellenbosch's terroir combines a unique blend of climate, soils, altitude, and topography, providing ideal conditions for grape growing and producing world-class wines with distinct character and complexity.

FOOD PAIRING:

Cape Town wines offer a diverse range of pairings just to name a few, Sauvignon Blanc's crisp acidity suits fresh seafood and salads; Chenin Blanc's versatility complements creamy pastas and Asian dishes; Shiraz/Syrah's bold flavors pair with grilled meats and game.

MALBEC
ARGENTINA | WINE TYPE: RED

Though originating in France, Argentina is now responsible for over 80% of the world's Malbec production! Characterized by deep inky colorization and jammy, meaty flavors, Malbec is now one of the world's go-to for a full-bodied red.

PRIMARY FLAVORS:

PLUM · BLACKBERRY · COCOA · CHERRY · TOBACCO

AROMAS:
Black Cherries, Chocolate, Blueberry, Plum.

FINISH:
Smoky and short.

PAIRS WELL WITH:
Red Meat, Blue Cheese, Roasted Peppers.

TASTE PROFILE:

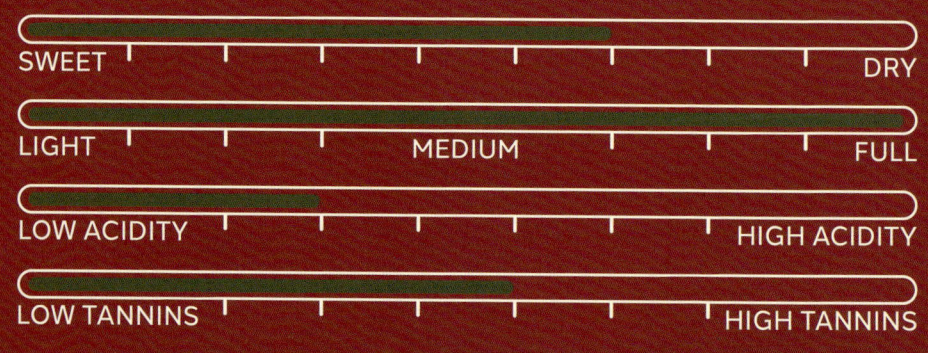

SWEET —————————————————— DRY
LIGHT —— MEDIUM —— FULL
LOW ACIDITY —————————————————— HIGH ACIDITY
LOW TANNINS —————————————————— HIGH TANNINS

HANDLE:

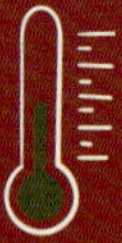

SERVE: 60-65°F / 15-18°C
GLASS TYPE: Burgundy
DECANT: 30-60 mins 
CELLAR: 5-15 years

FAMOUS FOR:

ITS APPROACHABLE, JUICY FRUIT FLAVORS AND A DEEP, RICH COLOR.

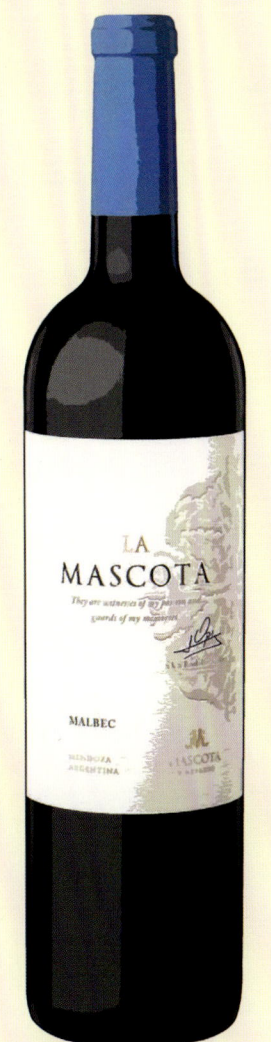

OUR TOP 15 WINES TO TRY!

WE RECOMMEND:
Mascota Vineyards La Mascota Malbec 2021

GRAPES:
Malbec

REGION:
Mendoza, Argentina

WINE STYLE:
Red

ALCOHOL CONTENT:
14%

PRICE:
£14-£17 | $14-$17

MERLOT
FRANCE | WINE TYPE: RED

The world's second-most prominent grape variety, Merlot has strong historic ties to Bordeaux, France, and is famous for its drinkability due to its fruity and less tannic structure!

PRIMARY FLAVORS:

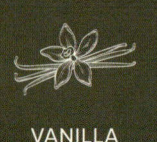

CHERRY PLUM BAY LEAF VANILLA CLOVES

AROMAS:
Strawberry, Cherry, Green Bell Pepper, Violet, Tobacco.

FINISH:
Soft tannins, ripe fruit flavors, savory undertones, subtle oak influence, balanced acidity.

PAIRS WELL WITH:
Tuna, Cured Meats, Caramelized Onions.

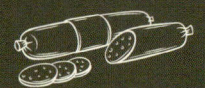

TASTE PROFILE:

SWEET •——————————————————————•—— DRY

LIGHT ————•—————————————— FULL (MEDIUM)

LOW ACIDITY ——•————————————————— HIGH ACIDITY

LOW TANNINS ———————•————————————— HIGH TANNINS

HANDLE:

SERVE
60–65°F/
15–18°C

GLASS TYPE
Standard Red

DECANT
30-60 mins

CELLAR
5-15 years

- 110 -

FAMOUS FOR:

BEING AN EASY-TO-DRINK WINE WITH GORGEOUS FRUIT NOTES AND A MID-WEIGHT BODY.

OUR TOP 15 WINES TO TRY!

WE RECOMMEND:
Res Fortes Wines Merlot Madness

GRAPES:
Merlot

REGION:
Côtes du Roussillon, France

WINE STYLE:
Red

ALCOHOL CONTENT:
13.5%

PRICE:
£14-£16 | $14-$35

PICPOUL DE PINET
FRANCE | WINE TYPE: WHITE

Balancing full flavors with a clean and crisp finish, making it a great alternative to Pinot Grigio and Sauvignon Blanc! Picpoul translates to 'stings the lip', relating to the wine's mineral acidity and dry, mouth-watering nature.

PRIMARY FLAVORS:

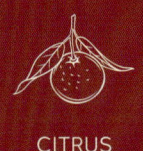

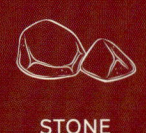

CITRUS | GREEN APPLE | PEAR | WHITE BLOSSOM | STONE

AROMAS:
Citrus, Flower Blossoms, Apricot, Apple.

FINISH:
Vibrant acidity, minerality, citrus flavors, subtle herbal undertones

PAIRS WELL WITH:
Goat's Cheese, Mussels, Bruschetta.

TASTE PROFILE:

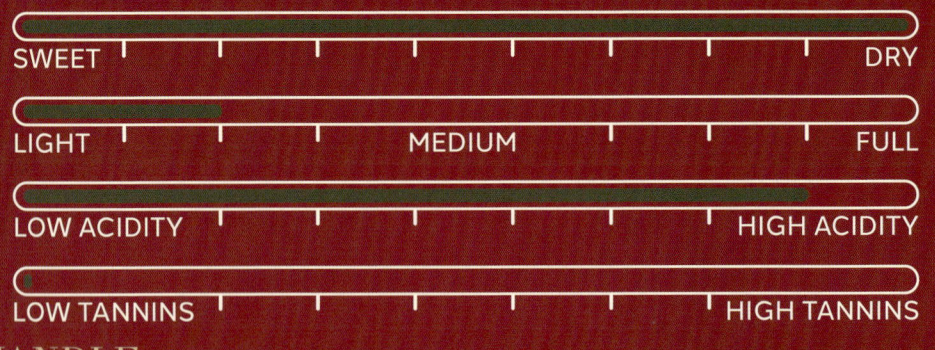

SWEET ———————————————————— DRY
LIGHT ———————————————————— FULL
LOW ACIDITY ———————————————————— HIGH ACIDITY
LOW TANNINS ———————————————————— HIGH TANNINS

HANDLE:

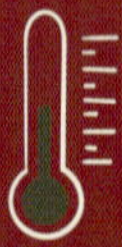

SERVE
46°-50°F/
8°-10°C

GLASS TYPE
Standard
White

DECANT
No

CELLAR
1-3 years

FAMOUS FOR:

ITS HIGH ACIDITY AND CRISP, GREEN APPLE FLAVORS.

OUR TOP 15 WINES TO TRY!

WE RECOMMEND:
Levre Piquante Picpoul de Pinet

GRAPES:
Picpoul

REGION:
Languedoc, France

WINE STYLE:
White

ALCOHOL CONTENT:
13%

PRICE:
£10-£14 | $17-$19

PINOT GRIGIO
ITALY | WINE TYPE: WHITE

Extremely popular and produced around the world, this wine originated in Burgundy under the French name, Pinot Gris. Gris refers to the grey-ish skin found on this grape variety, however as Italy is now the biggest producer of this wine, it is mostly referred to as Pinot Grigio, its Italian name!

PRIMARY FLAVORS:

| LEMON | PEAR | NECTARINE | APPLE | LIME |

AROMAS:
Honeysuckle, White Flower, Wet Stone, Pear.

FINISH:
Clean, crisp, and invigorating, with vibrant acidity, citrus flavors.

PAIRS WELL WITH:
Seafood, Salads, Pad Thai.

TASTE PROFILE:

SWEET —————————————————— DRY
LIGHT ————— MEDIUM ————— FULL
LOW ACIDITY —————————————— HIGH ACIDITY
LOW TANNINS —————————————— HIGH TANNINS

HANDLE:

SERVE
45-49°F/
7-9°C

GLASS TYPE
Standard White

DECANT
No

CELLAR
No

FAMOUS FOR:

BEING LIGHT, REFRESHING, AND WIDELY ACCESSIBLE – PERFECT ON A SUNNY DAY!

OUR TOP 15 WINES TO TRY!

WE RECOMMEND:
Friuli Colli Orientali DOC Pinot Grigio 2022 Sirch

GRAPES:
Pinot Grigio

REGION:
Veneto, Italy

WINE STYLE:
White

ALCOHOL CONTENT:
13%

PRICE:
£11-£14 | $9-$12

PRIMITIVO
ITALY | WINE TYPE: RED

Famous for producing dark, tannic, and slightly spiced wines, Primitivo is known as an Italian red grape, but originated in Croatia. In the US, this grape is commonly referred to as Zinfandel, especially when grown in US soil!

PRIMARY FLAVORS:

RASPBERRY | **PEPPER** | **PLUM** | **CHERRY** | **CINNAMON**

AROMAS:
Cinnamon, Blackberry, Dried Plum, Cherry.

FINISH:
Bold and robust qualities, with rich tannins, dark fruit flavors, spice

PAIRS WELL WITH:
Tagine, Roasted Peppers, Halloumi.

TASTE PROFILE:

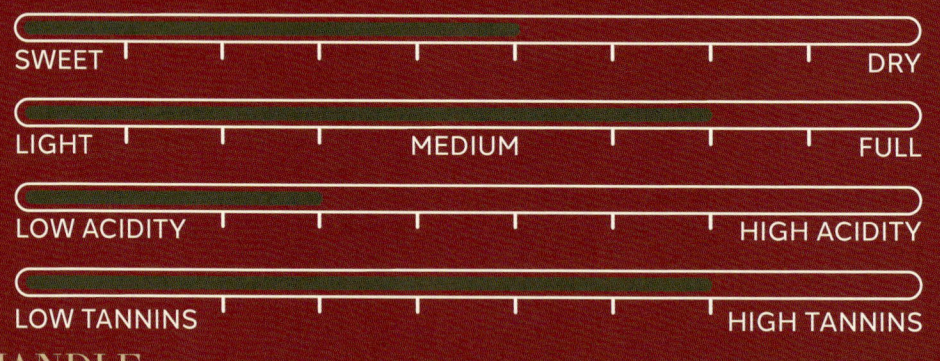

SWEET —————————————— DRY
LIGHT —————————————— FULL
LOW ACIDITY —————————————— HIGH ACIDITY
LOW TANNINS —————————————— HIGH TANNINS

HANDLE:

SERVE
61-65°F/
16-18°C

GLASS TYPE
Universal

DECANT
30 mins

CELLAR
10-15 years

FAMOUS FOR:
HAVING BOLD, JAMMY NOTES AND WARMING SPICE NOTES.

OUR TOP 15 WINES TO TRY!

WE RECOMMEND:
Primitivo di Manduria DOC Riserva 2020 Doppio Passo

GRAPES:
Primitivo

REGION:
Puglia, Italy

WINE STYLE:
Red

ALCOHOL CONTENT:
14.5%

PRICE:
£10-£15 | $10-$15

PROVENCE ROSÉ
FRANCE | WINE TYPE: PALE ROSÉ

Unlike other sweeter forms of rosé, Provence rosés are usually found to be dry and crisp, with a fruity and minerally flavor. Many Provence rosés have an AOC label, which means that wine using that name must fit within certain regulations, similar to Champagne!

PRIMARY FLAVORS:

| ROSE | GRAPEFRUIT | STRAWBERRY | WHITE PEACH | CITRUS |

AROMAS:
Lemon Zest, Rose, Strawberry, Melon, White Pepper.

FINISH:
Bright acidity, delicate fruit flavors, minerality, clean and crisp.

PAIRS WELL WITH:
Risotto, Pasta, Smoked Salmon.

TASTE PROFILE:

SWEET ———————————————— DRY
LIGHT ———————————————— FULL
LOW ACIDITY ———————————————— HIGH ACIDITY
LOW TANNINS ———————————————— HIGH TANNINS

HANDLE:

- **SERVE:** 38–45°F / 3–7°C
- **GLASS TYPE:** Standard White
- **DECANT:** No
- **CELLAR:** No

FAMOUS FOR:

PROVIDING A DRIER, MINERAL-DRIVEN ROSÉ OPTION.

OUR TOP 15 WINES TO TRY!

WE RECOMMEND:
Côtes de Provence AOC Réserve des Templiers 2022 Château Peyrassol

GRAPES:
Grenache, Cinsault and Vermentino

REGION:
Provence, France

WINE STYLE:
Rosé

ALCOHOL CONTENT:
12,5%

PRICE:
£19-£24 | $25-$27

SYRAH (SHIRAZ)

AUSTRALIA | WINE TYPE: RED

Originating in the Rhône Valley of France, Syrah is now the most planted grape of Australia, where it is famously called Shiraz. This wine is rich, meaty, and powerful – perfect for a decadent evening!

PRIMARY FLAVORS:

- PLUM
- BLACK PEPPERCORN
- BLUEBERRY
- TOBACCO
- OAK

AROMAS:
Blackberry, Coffee, Pepper, Smoke, Floral.

FINISH:
Velvety tannins, dark fruit flavors, spice and pepper notes.

PAIRS WELL WITH:
Rich Spices, BBQ Vegetables, Stew.

TASTE PROFILE:

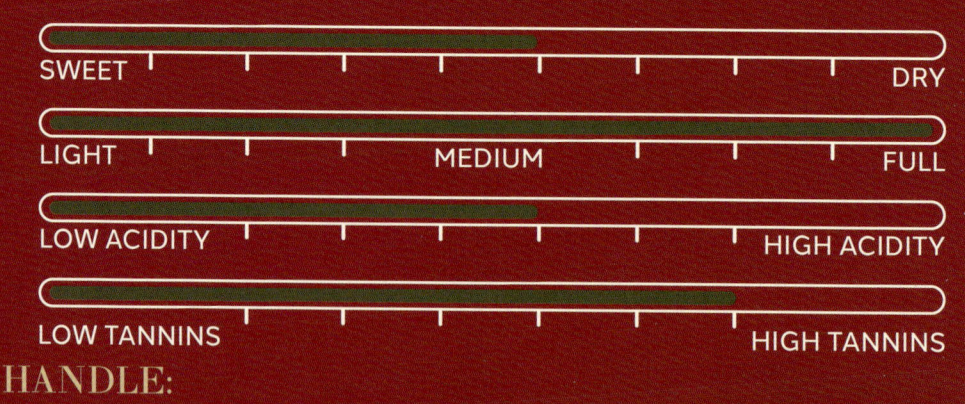

SWEET —————————————————— DRY

LIGHT —————— MEDIUM —————— FULL

LOW ACIDITY —————————— HIGH ACIDITY

LOW TANNINS —————————— HIGH TANNINS

HANDLE:

SERVE
60–68°F/
15–20°C

GLASS TYPE
Standard Red

DECANT
1 hr

CELLAR
5–10 years

FAMOUS FOR:

ITS RICH, DARK FRUIT TASTE, AND SAVORY, EARTHY NOTES

OUR TOP 15 WINES TO TRY!

WE RECOMMEND:
Barossa Valley Shiraz The Barossan 2020 Peter Lehmann

GRAPES:
Syrah/Shiraz

REGION:
Barossa Valley, South Australia

WINE STYLE:
Red

ALCOHOL CONTENT:
14,5%

PRICE:
£15-£19 | $13-$21

TEMPRANILLO
SPAIN | WINE TYPE: RED

Spain's number one red grape, Tempranillo is at the heart of Spain's famous Rioja region, and is versatile and complex! It is a popular blending wine, and is even used in the process of Port, and whilst it lacks the body of other reds, it is a complex and flavorful wine.

PRIMARY FLAVORS:

| CHERRY | CEDAR | FIG | STRAWBERRY | TOBACCO |

AROMAS:
Strawberry, Chocolate, Leather, Plum, Cherry.

FINISH:
Smooth tannins, red fruit flavors, earthy undertones, oak influence

PAIRS WELL WITH:
Manchego, Paella, Enchiladas.

TASTE PROFILE:

SWEET ———————————————— DRY

LIGHT ——————— MEDIUM ——————— FULL

LOW ACIDITY ———————————————— HIGH ACIDITY

LOW TANNINS ———————————————— HIGH TANNINS

HANDLE:

SERVE
60–68°F/
15–20°C

GLASS TYPE
Standard Red

DECANT
1 hr

CELLAR
5-10 years

FAMOUS FOR:

ITS BOLD, STRUCTURED, INTENSE FRUIT FLAVORS AND FIRM TANNINS.

OUR TOP 15 WINES TO TRY!

WE RECOMMEND:
Ribera del Duero Tempranillo DO
Finca Resalso 2021 Emilio Moro

GRAPES:
Tempranillo

REGION:
Castile, Spain

WINE STYLE:
Red

ALCOHOL CONTENT:
13%

PRICE:
£14-£17 | $13-$15

VERMENTINO
ITALY | WINE TYPE: WHITE

Predominantly grown in Sardinia and Tuscany, Vermentino is a light-bodied white wine that is very complex, and is likened to Sauvignon Blanc. Due to its slight obscurity when compared to other whites, this can also be a great value option!

PRIMARY FLAVORS:

LEMON **LIME** **GRAPEFRUIT** **ALMOND** **PEAR**

AROMAS:
Apple, Honey, Papaya, Pear.

FINISH:
Vibrant acidity, citrus and stone fruit flavors.

PAIRS WELL WITH:
Light Meats, White Fish, Citrus.

TASTE PROFILE:

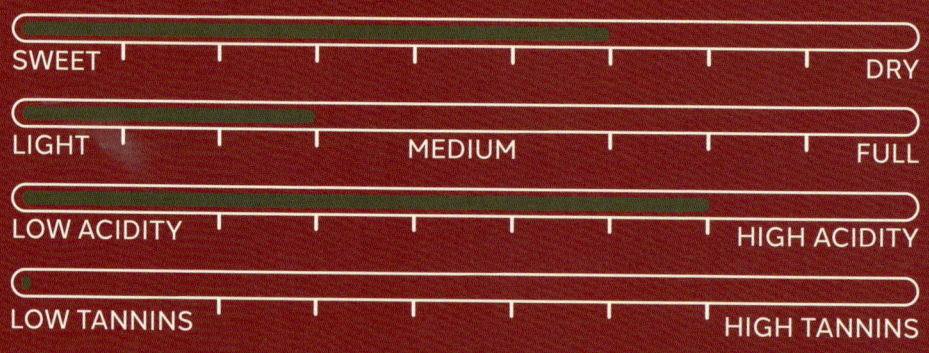

SWEET ———————————————————— DRY

LIGHT ———————————————————— FULL (MEDIUM)

LOW ACIDITY ———————————————————— HIGH ACIDITY

LOW TANNINS ———————————————————— HIGH TANNINS

HANDLE:

SERVE
45–55°F / 7–12°C

GLASS TYPE
Standard White

DECANT
No

CELLAR
No

FAMOUS FOR:
ITS DELICIOUSLY COMPLEX, CRISP, AND PACKED WITH FLAVOR.

OUR TOP 15 WINES TO TRY!

WE RECOMMEND:
Colli di Luni DOC Cavagino 2022 Lunae

GRAPES:
Vermentino

REGION:
Liguria, Italy

WINE STYLE:
White

ALCOHOL CONTENT:
14%

PRICE:
£16-£25 | $21-$25

VIOGNIER
AUSTRALIA | WINE TYPE: WHITE

Known for its highly aromatic profile and robust texture, this is a rich and oily white. Often produced in oak, it has a richness similar to Chardonnay, and is growing in popularity in vineyards in California and Australia.

PRIMARY FLAVORS:

| MANGO | ORANGE | PEACH | HONEYSUCKLE | ROSE |

AROMAS:
Apricot, Apple, Peach, Ginger.

FINISH:
Intense stone fruit flavors, floral aromas, citrus notes, spice.

PAIRS WELL WITH:
Cured Meats, Chicken, Shellfish.

TASTE PROFILE:

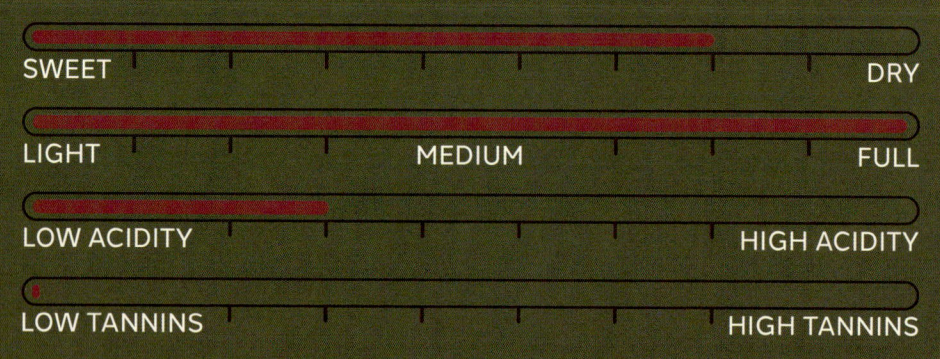

SWEET ──────────────────────────── DRY

LIGHT ──────── MEDIUM ──────── FULL

LOW ACIDITY ──────────────────── HIGH ACIDITY

LOW TANNINS ──────────────────── HIGH TANNINS

HANDLE:

SERVE
50–55°F/
10–13°C

GLASS TYPE
Standard White

DECANT
No

CELLAR
No

FAMOUS FOR:

ITS FULL BODY AND FLORAL AROMAS.

OUR TOP 15 WINES TO TRY!

WE RECOMMEND:
McLaren Vale Viognier Marsanne GI The Hermit Crab 2021 D'Arenberg

GRAPES:
Viognier, Marsanne 50%

REGION:
Barossa Valley, South Australia

WINE STYLE:
White

ALCOHOL CONTENT:
13%

PRICE:
£13-£15 | $15-$17

GO FROM SIPPER TO SOMMELIER

As we close the pages on this compact wine guide – remember that your sommelier journey is not over yet! You have learned the notes and aromas, and other features of some of the world's best and most popular wines. Which stole the show for you? What are you looking for in your favorite sips?

But the fun doesn't stop here! Keep swirling and sipping with the wisdom of a seasoned wine connoisseur. Remember that every bottle tells a story, and you can continue to taste the world from the comfort of a wine glass! Let's toast to your next pour as your sommelier journey continues!